IDEOLOGIES
OF
POLITICS

Edited by

ANTHONY DE CRESPIGNY

and

JEREMY CRONIN

CAPE TOWN

⟩RD UNIVERSITY PRESS

NEW YORK

Oxford University Press

OXFORD   LONDON   GLASGOW
NEW YORK   TORONTO   MELBOURNE   WELLINGTON
IBADAN   NAIROBI   DAR ES SALAAM   CAPE TOWN
KUALA LUMPUR   SINGAPORE   JAKARTA   HONG KONG   TOKYO
DELHI   BOMBAY   CALCUTTA   MADRAS   KARACHI

Editors' introduction and this arrangement
copyright © 1975 Oxford University Press Southern Africa

2nd Impression 1978

ISBN 0 19 570070 8

Printed in South Africa by Citadel Press, Lansdowne, Cape
Published by Oxford University Press, Harrington House,
Barrack Street, Cape Town 8001, South Africa

Contents

Acknowledgements

Acknowledgement is made to the following for permission to use works which are their copyright:

Methuen & Co. Ltd. for 'On being Conservative' by Michael Oakeshott from *Rationalism in Politics and Other Essays*, 1962.

Oxford University Press, Oxford for 'What is Socialism?' by G. D. H. Cole from *Political Studies* Vol I, 1953 and for 'Reflections on Totalitarianism' by Robert Orr from *Political Studies* Vol. 21, 1973.

Instituto di Scienze Politiche, University of Pavia, for 'The Principles of a Liberal Social Order' by F. A. Hayek from *Il Politico* December 1966.

Journal of the History of Ideas for 'Democracy' by Richard Wollheim from the *Journal of the History of Ideas*, Vol. 19 (1958), pp. 225-242.

Macmillan Publishing Co. Inc. for 'Nationalism' by Hans Kohn from *International Encyclopaedia of the Social Sciences*, ed. David L. Sills, Vol. II, pp. 63-70. Copyright © 1968 by Crowell Collier and Macmillan, Inc.

Introduction

The nomads of the desert, said Jean-Jacques Rousseau, reflecting on the close connection between language and mode of life, have a hundred different words for a camel. It is tempting to assert that with the word 'ideology' in our times the converse is the case; one word and many realities, and it is the word that has become a beast of burden. Yet, in its way, the point Rousseau was trying to establish still holds, for the diverse senses of 'ideology' tell us much about the wanderings of our own recent history.

The load of meanings that it carries is not exactly surprising. The term 'ideology' is, after all, itself thoroughly ideologized and if this statement makes some sense, and surely it does, then the term is not so vague as to be without the core of a meaning. There are probably two features, at least, that are commonly to be found in most contemporary uses of 'ideology'. First, it usually designates a system of beliefs or attitudes that is held by a social group. The nature of social groups that are thus linked with ideologies varies with the political and sociological persuasions of the particular social analyst. Secondly, it is normally implied that these beliefs or attitudes need to be assessed, not so much on their own terms, as by the practical effects or social interests they tend to promote. The real import of an ideology is more symptomatic than literal. Here again there is much variation when it comes to details; there are those who hold that ideologies obtain, or aspire to obtain, their effects entirely through distortion, whereas others employ the term in a more neutral fashion.

If we leave aside, for the moment, these contemporary differences, and if we retain what at least seems to be the core of a meaning (viz. that ideologies are systems of practically orientated beliefs and attitudes associated with social groups), then it is clear that theoretical interest in this general reality is somewhat older than the actual term 'ideology' itself. Bacon's criticism, in the *Novum Organum*, of 'idola' – idols or preconceptions that deceive men and constitute obstacles in the path of true knowledge – has sometimes been cited as one of the earliest theoretical probes into the general domain of ideology. Bacon regarded 'idola' as being predominantly the consequence of man's psychological make-up, but he did also partly attribute them to social factors.[1]

It is doubtful whether there is an unbroken line of descent in the European intellectual tradition running from Bacon's 'idola' to the modern conception of ideology. We certainly do owe a great deal, however, to the seventeenth and eighteenth centuries, and particularly to the writers of the French Enlightenment. In many ways ideology (although the term was not yet used) was the central concern of the *philosophes*. They were fascinated, and alarmed, by the way in which nations and indeed whole epochs could be circumscribed by systems of belief. Europe had become enmeshed in illusory traditions that were distilled and promoted, so the *philosophes* believed, by despots and their allies, the priest caste, in order to maintain the masses in ignorant slumber. Descartes' methodical doubt, Montesquieu's travelling Persians, Rousseau's state of nature, like Robinson Crusoe's shipwreck, were so many devices designed to loosen the grip of the familiar, to break the spell of prejudice.

When it first began its career, 'ideology' enjoyed a sense rather different from that of today. The term was first coined at the time of the French Revolution by Destutt de Tracy. De Tracy and his circle of intellectuals associated with the Institut de France were liberals, and philosophers in the mainstream of of an intellectual tradition that runs from Descartes through to the more or less solitary, contemporary figure of Sartre. One of the features of this tradition has been (to use the English title of one of Sartre's works) – 'The Search for a Method', the quest for a philosopher's stone that will transform the mundane, not into gold but knowledge. *Idéologie* was the name that de Tracy gave to the particular method that he proposed as universally applicable. *Idéologie*, or the science of ideas, was to provide the true foundation for all other sciences. Its own particular domain was 'the natural history of the mind'; it was to investigate and describe the manner in which our thoughts are constituted.

'Ideology' acquired a connotation more familiar to us when Napoleon and the liberals of the Institute fell out. When the liberals stood in the way of his centralizing policies Napoleon dismissed them as mere ideologists. Ideology was lost in a fog of abstract ideas, hopelessly searching for first principles. 'Cannon killed feudalism. Ink will kill modern society'.[2]

'Ideology' as an accusation, used in contrast with all that is supposed to be realistic; this is, of course, one of the senses in which the word is still employed today. Its more encompassing sense, to characterize the belief-systems of social groups, is of even more recent origin, dating back to the 1840s and the early writings of Marx. He was certainly not the first to notice that social groups carry with them systems of outlooks, often more implicit than explicit, systems that limit conceptual horizons and influence not only the answers men find but also the very questions they tend to ask. In this regard Marx was particularly indebted to Hegel, but it was Marx who attached the word 'ideology' to these social belief-systems and with the spread of his ideas this sense of the word has become more general.

Although Marx and Engels remain more or less faithful to this overall usage, there are many specific variations from the *1844 Manuscripts* through *The German Ideology* to the later works. Within the Marxist tradition, in consequence, there have been several different approaches to the question of ideology, differences that have grown out of the shifts and variations within the texts of Marx and Engels. It is possible to distinguish three different interpretations, all claiming allegiance to Marxism – (1) ideology as 'false consciousness'; (2) ideology as a reflection of the economic infrastructure; and (3) ideology as an organic and necessary part of all societies.

(1) Following Marx's relatively early work, *The German Ideology* (1845), some writers have depicted ideology as a deformed and inverted reflection of the real. It is conceived as a pure emptiness, an illusion that is ignorant of its own material foundations. Clearly this view leads to a restrictive definition of ideology. The boundaries of ideology are constituted by what it is not: knowledge, 'true consciousness'. The position adopted by G. Lukács, in his *History and Class Consciousness*, is one of

the clearest developments in this line. Lukács defines ideology as 'false consciousness'. Its falsity lies primarily in its partiality; it is unable to seize the 'total meaning' of society and history. Lukács contrasts ideology with 'true consciousness', the bearer of which is, as we might expect, the proletarian class. Within its own self-consciousness the proletariat, the universal class according to Lukács, carries the knowledge of the total socio-historical process. The imminent victory of the proletariat will, supposedly, abolish all particular standpoints. Lukács' position here contrasts with Lenin's espousal of science, for to identify 'false consciousness' with all partial or restricted outlooks is to cast doubt on the specialization that any science necessarily implies. Lukács has been joined, on this point, by such thinkers as Marcuse, Sartre and Habermas who all criticize specialization in the name of some 'totalizing consciousness'. This idea of a 'total consciousness' owes, perhaps, more to Hegel than to Marx, and indeed the general structure of Lukács' *History and Class Consciousness* is very Hegelian. Hegel's Absolute Spirit is simply replaced with a new Subject of History, the proletariat. Not surprisingly, therefore, this work of Lukács has met with considerable approbation from the neo-Hegelian Frankfurt school.

(2) The interpretation of ideology as a mere reflection of the economic infrastructure is most clearly typified by the writings of Bernstein. In the name of an anti-Hegelianism, ideology is reduced by Bernstein to an epiphenomenon, a mechanical reflection of the movement of the economic base. Ideology obediently follows the fatalistic unfolding of history, without itself possessing any real potency. Ideology comes to be massively depoliticized. The prevalence of this view of ideology amongst Marxists in Germany in the 1920s and 1930s has been seen, by some writers, as the root cause of the inability of the German socialists to confront the ideological onslaught of the Nazis.[3]

(3) A third tradition within Marxism, to which Gramsci and, more recently, Althusser have in particular contributed, portrays ideology neither as simply the False, nor as a mere echo of something else. Both Gramsci an Althusser depict ideology as being more than a system of ideas; ideology for them has, so to

speak, a material existence within such social institutions as the church, the school, the family and the political party. Ideology is articulated and acquired within the practices of these institutions. Rather than being primarily a conscious formulation, it functions as a veritable unconscious. It determines types of behaviour and habits, it is 'organic', it organizes men and reproduces social relations. Both Gramsci and Althusser view ideology not as a contingent excrescence arising at a certain point in history and confined to certain classes, but as a necessary component of all societies. It forms men and places them in a state in which they are able to respond to the exigencies of their conditions of existence. Man is – says Althusser, adjusting somewhat Aristotle's maxim – an ideological animal.

It should be said, however, that for Althusser ideology is not the only form of thought. In his view there is a sharp division between ideology and the sciences. The sciences are constituted only through a theoretical activity that produces a 'break' with the ideological. Ideology, says Althusser, is the imaginary form in which individuals give a centre to their relationship with their real conditions of existence. Through ideology they live this relationship as subjects, whereas the discourse of the sciences is essentially de-centred; the sciences are, and must be, subjectless.

Marxists are far from having an intellectual monopoly over the term 'ideology'. The question of ideology has, in recent times, also been linked with the Sociology of Knowledge, and with the works of Karl Mannheim. According to Mannheim most modes of thought cannot be properly understood without being situated within their social context. The conclusions of logic and mathematics, when validly deduced, are universally true, but with the social sciences, and possibly with the natural sciences (Mannheim vacillates here), the conclusions reached are only true for groups of people who are similarly situated, who approach the matter in question from the same social perspective. Mannheim directs much polemic against the ruggedly individualistic assumptions of classical epistemology. He argues that individuals do not develop ideas on their own. The perspective that informs an individual's ideas, the very questions that he asks, are the products of social circumstance.

Mannheim's standpoint gives rise, as we might expect, to a predicament: what is the status of this sociological theory that pronounces that all such theory is relative? This predicament has come to be known, appropriately, as Mannheim's Paradox. To save his own theory Mannheim must insist, and he does, that because a mode of thought is socially determined it is not necessarily thereby condemned to falsity. What a theory says may well be the product of a particular class interest, for instance, and yet it may still be true. This gives Mannheim some breathing space, but he still needs to go further in order to ground his own theory. He tries, in consequence, like Lukács, to locate a particular social group that will, by its very style of life, be prone to truth. For Lukács, as we have seen, the proletariat was the candidate; Mannheim plumps for the intelligentsia. If all social theory is the product of particular social perspectives, then that social stratum whose style of life is least entrenched within one perspective or another, has the best chance of perceiving some truths. The intelligentsia in the modern world, an 'unattached middle stratum', 'unanchored' and 'relatively classless' is, so we are told, admirably suited to the call of truth. Thus Mannheim's own theory, the product of a member of this social stratum, holds itself hopefully above the swamp of blind relativism.

Whether the modern intelligentsia is unattached or unanchored is open to question, but certainly these epithets can be applied to Mannheim's use of the term 'ideology'. He is anything but consistent on this score. It is true that he does show some concern for definitional clarity when he distinguishes between two possible uses of the term, between what he calls the 'particular conception of ideology', and the 'total conception of ideology'. In the particular conception ideology is used simply as a negative evaluation. An opponent's arguments (or part of them) are regarded as ideological, they are dismissed as lies or errors. This view of ideology, says Mannheim, has more affinity with a psychological than a sociological dimension. With the total conception of ideology we are much more concerned with world outlooks, with the belief-systems of an age or of an historical, social group. Unfortunately it is sometimes unclear as to whether Mannheim is using the term in its particular or total application. What is more, he is capable of using the term in senses that are not exactly reducible to either the particular or total conceptions. At times, for instance, 'ideology' means conservative as contrasted with utopian thinking.[4] Mannheim is not unaware of his ambivalent usage; he attempts to argue at one point that there is some merit in his refusal to be clear about what he means by 'ideology'.[5] Flexibility, the supposed social virtue of the intelligentsia, is so esteemed by Mannheim that it invades even his use of concepts.

In contemporary American social theory the term 'ideology' has normally been reserved for consciously formulated, political outlooks. Within this general perspective there has been, once more, a great deal of variation; ranging from Shils, who associates 'ideology' with rabid, fanatical closed systems (principally typified by communism and fascism), through to more or less neutral applications of the term. For Shils ideologies are 'the creations of charismatic persons who possess powerful, expansive, and simplified visions of the world'.[6] Ideologies are always opposed to the status quo, even where their advocates happen to be in power. Shils' view of ideology is simply repeated in all but its trappings by some American New Left circles, which depict ideology as the cunning construct of big-business moguls and their political lieutenants.

Geertz, in an important article,[7] has argued for a more neutral conception of ideology – neutral as to its particular, political complexion as well as to its veracity. Ideology, according to Geertz, is usefully seen as one of the forms of cultural pattern which provide practical orientations whereby individuals are able to accord some coherence to their social circumstance. Although ideologies tend to be schematic, precisely because of their practical function, the schematization does not necessarily lead to serious distortion. It is not distortion but function which is the defining characteristic of ideology. For Geertz ideologies are, nevertheless, the deliberate constructions of individuals, or small groups of individuals. Ideologies are distinguished from what he calls (in rather quaint, if not very rigorous, Burkean terms) the 'untaught feelings', 'the unexamined prejudices' of stable societies. For this reason ideology, in Geertz's view, plays a major role in areas in which there is rapid social transformation, such as in the Third World today, while its impact is only marginal in the more established centres.

With ideology, then, we are confronted with a concept that is sufficiently useful as to be a pity to lose. Yet it is a concept that cannot be employed with impunity unless careful clarifications are made. Perhaps the most significant step in this regard is to distinguish two levels within the ideological. This is a point that has been suggested in different ways by several different writers. The American, William T. Bluhm, for instance, calls for a distinction between 'forensic ideologies' and 'latent ideologies':

> 'Forensic ideologies' are the elaborate, self-conscious word systems, formulated at a rather abstract level, which constitute the language of political discussion in times of severe stress and strain. 'Latent ideologies' are the implicit sets of political words which are expressed in attitude and behaviour during more settled times, but which can be 'excavated' – that is, raised to the forensic level – by social research.[8]

A similar, if not entirely equivalent view, is to be found in Plamenatz's distinction between 'sophisticated' and 'unsophisticated' ideology, and in Althusser's distinction between 'ideology' and 'theoretical ideology', the latter being the consciously worked-up formulation of unconscious ideological attitudes.[9]

The great advantage of retaining the word 'ideology' for both levels is that this underlines conceptually the essential connection between the 'latent' and the 'forensic'. Writers who confine, in effect, the term 'ideology' simply to 'forensic', political belief-systems, to systems that are framed by individuals or small groups of individuals, tend to overlook the close connection that these have with more deepseated cultural patterns. Political beliefs like communism or fascism tend, in consequence, to be explained away as the pathological products of a few satanic minds. On the other hand, the distinction between 'forensic' and 'latent' serves, as Bluhm correctly asserts, to overcome a misunderstanding that was particularly rife in the fifties and early sixties, at the height of the 'end of ideology' debate. The debate was between those who argued that we had entered an age in which ideology was outmoded and those who argued that ideology was a perennial phenomenon. In fact much of the debate was misdirected since the two camps were often using the term 'ideology' differently. Those who argued that the age of ideology was over tended to equate 'ideology' with particular 'forensic' political creeds; whereas those who argued that it was an inevitable social reality were according 'ideology' a much wider connotation, more akin to the notion of an implicit belief-system.

* * * *

Turning from the general to the particular and to the essays which comprise this collection, it should be stressed immediately that ideologies are very variously understood and that one is on firmer ground in speaking of Oakeshott's conservatism or Hayek's liberalism than in speaking of conservatism or liberalism *tout court*. The same or apparently equivalent words vary in their meanings both within and between different countries, from time to time and in the writings of particular theorists. It would be a formidable undertaking to try to map out variations in use in differing contexts, particularly since one would have to take account of emotive as well as descriptive meaning. But a reading of the essays reprinted here should sufficiently indicate the dimensions of the problem. However, it would be wrong to conclude from the fact that the words used to refer to ideologies are employed in a confusing variety of senses, that they are therefore devoid of meaning. While, for instance, there is not just one conception of liberalism, there is a family of conceptions, united by points of resemblance if not by a set of common features.

It is evident that while the ideologies presented or discussed in this book differ they are not necessarily incompatible. Everything will depend on the way they are conceived. Hayek, for example, regards his conception of liberalism as being compatible with democracy in its insistence that the majority should determine what is law, but as conflicting with democracy where the democrat believes that the majority determines what is *good* law. On the other hand, Hayek's liberalism is unqualifiedly incompatible with socialism and totalitarianism. But let us glance at each essay in turn in order to see how its author conceives of a particular ideology, whether he recognizes subdivisions within it, and whether he distinguishes one ideology from another.

Oakeshott's conservatism presents immediate problems partly because there has been some doubt as to whether he is a conservative and partly because he would certainly not want to call himself an ideologist. As for the latter problem it need only be said that he is not an ideologist in *his* sense; as for the appropriateness of the label 'conservative', it is sufficient to say that he is a conservative if 'conservatism' is taken in its usual sense as the preference for customs and institutions which have grown up over a long period. As Oakeshott writes:

> To be conservative . . . is to prefer the familiar to the unknown, to prefer the tried to the untried, fact to mystery, the actual to the possible, the limited to the unbounded, the near to the distant, the sufficient to the superabundant, the convenient to the perfect, present laughter to utopian bliss.[10]

Oakeshott's sympathy for conservatism as a disposition is obvious. However, his conservatism is idiosyncratic since it is not at all tied to any of the general ideas which are typically produced when conservatism is explained or defended – religious beliefs of some kind, an organic view of human society, a natural right to private property, the absolute value of free human choice, innate selfishness, and so on. For Oakeshott, a disposition to be politically conservative is tied only to a certain view of the customary activity of governing: '. . . governing is recognized as a specific and limited activity; not the management of an enterprise, but the rule of those engaged in a great diversity of self-chosen enterprises'.[11] The business of government is not to impose substantive activities but to enable people to pursue their self-chosen activities with the minimum of frustration. It is concerned with activities but only in respect of 'their propensity to collide'.

Oakeshott's conservatism, then, is without theoretical foundations. If a man of conservative disposition should be asked to justify his view that governments should simply accept the current diversity of beliefs and activities, it suffices for him to reply: 'Why not? Their dreams are no different from those of anyone else; and if it is boring to have to listen to dreams of others being recounted, it is insufferable to be forced to re-enact them'.[12]

While admitting that liberals of his kind have much to learn from some conservatives – and he would include Oakeshott – Hayek does not call himself a 'conservative'. For his resistance to such a description there are three main reasons. First, his liberalism has theoretical foundations and therefore knows where it wishes to go, whereas for Hayek 'true' conservatism cannot by its very nature offer an alternative to the prevailing direction of movement. Secondly, conservatives are fearful of change, suspicious of the new as such, while Hayek's brand of liberalism is based on a willingness to let change run its course even though we cannot know precisely where it will lead. And thirdly, Hayek is critical of a conservative tendency to be autho-ritarian and anti-democratic.[13]

The essence of Hayek's liberalism can be summed up in a quotation from the essay which appears here:

Liberalism ... derives from the discovery of a self-generating or spontaneous order in social affairs . . . , an order which [makes] it possible to utilize the knowledge and skill of all members of society to a much greater extent than would be possible in any order created by central direction, and [reflects] the consequent desire to make as full use of these powerful spontaneous ordering forces as possible.[14]

Hayek is emphatic in distinguishing his kind of liberalism from what now goes by this name in the United States. While Hayek emphasizes freedom from legal restraints contemporary American liberals view freedom as participation and effective choice and are much closer to the 'constructivist rationalism' of Voltaire and Rousseau. While Hayek sets strict limits to and is deeply suspicious of the powers of *all* government, American liberalism today is *étatiste* and looks to the interventions of *democratic* government for distributive justice and social pro-gress. While Hayek stresses the beneficial social effects of evolu-tion and spontaneous order, American liberals seek a radical reconstruction of society on the basis of deliberate design.

The foremost historian of socialist thought, the late G. D. H. Cole, has great difficulty in answering the question 'What is Socialism?' in contemporary terms. He does not provide a definition of 'socialism' and indeed states that the term cannot be defined since socialism has taken so many diverse forms in different countries and under the influence of different exponents. Two essential elements are an emphasis on 'the need for collective regulation of social and economic affairs' and a 'thorough-going hostility to class-divisions'. But neither of these elements adequately distinguishes socialism from all other ideologies. It may be added that socialism stands for 'democracy', but this is not very helpful since there are different conceptions of democracy.

Cole distinguishes four sorts of socialism – utopian, scientific, anarchist and evolutionary – but would agree that the thought of particular socialists often includes aspects of more than one sort of socialism. Cole's principal contrast is between the utopian socialism of men like Owen and Fourier and the 'scientific' socialism of Marx.

> Where most of the early Socialists [the Utopians] differed from the Marxists . . . was . . . in resting their case on arguments of justice and human brotherhood rather than on a conception of class-*power*. Marx's 'scientific' socialism was an attempt to demonstrate the certainty of the conquest of power by the working class quite apart from any consideration of what *ought* to happen, in a moral sense.[15]

The socialist anarchists accepted Marx's view that socialism must come about by way of class-conflict, but rejected power as the basis of the new social order. They were 'utopians' only in the sense that they thought the millenium would occur once 'capitalism' and its upholder, the state, had been destroyed. Evolutionary socialists, such as Bernstein and the English Fabians, differed from most Marxists not in repudiating the materialist conception of history, but in believing that under responsible government and a broad franchise, socialism could be accomplished through the electoral process.

In his essay on democracy Wollheim differentiates four types of question that arise in contemporary discussions – the meaning, conditions and justification of democracy, and the relation between democracy and other political concepts. We shall leave aside his discussion of the second and third types of question.

If 'democracy' is taken to mean 'rule of the people' two questions immediately present themselves: how is it possible for the people, being so numerous, to rule and, supposing that it were, who would be left to be ruled? Wollheim distinguishes two ways of answering these questions in democratic thought, one metaphysical and the other empiricist. According to the former, we possess two selves: a 'true' self and an 'arbitrary' self. While the demands of arbitrary selves are at variance, those of true selves are necessarily in harmony. Applying this distinction, the two questions have been answered by saying (a) that the people can be said to rule when their true, necessarily concordant, selves rule, and (b) that they are ruled when their true selves rule their arbitrary selves. However, as Wollheim observes, this proposed solution to the problem is confronted, among other difficulties, by the apparent impossibility of recognizing what are the demands of true selves.

Turning to the empiricist solution, the questions are answered by saying (a) that the people, though numerous and diverse, can rule in the sense of exerting some power over the use of supreme legislative and executive powers; and (b) that they can be ruled since these powers 'can be controlled *by* a group of people and yet also exercised *over* that group'.[16] But while Wollheim greatly prefers this solution to the 'idealist' alternative he does say that it has to resolve practical difficulties resulting from 'diversities and disharmonies' in society. For if, as seems likely, there is disagreement about the use of supreme legislative and executive powers, how can the people control the use of such powers? This problem is practical rather than logical, since there is no difficulty about saying that the people control policy even when a particular policy is not universally approved.

Wollheim discusses at some length the relation between democracy and socialism. He refers to the Marxist tendency to alter radically the descriptive meaning of the word 'democracy' whilst taking full advantage of its laudatory emotive meaning, and to the position of those democratic socialists who argue that democracy involves popular control of economic as well as political institutions. Wollheim also mentions those 'conservatives' who contend that democracy and socialism are mutually incompatible. In this connection Hayek is cited as an example.

While democracy and totalitarianism are often thought of as opposites, it is in principle possible, as Hayek observes, that a democratic government might be totalitarian. This can be seen if we take Wollheim's 'idealist' tradition of democratic thought and assume that only a highly gifted leader, or group of leaders, is capable of discerning the demands of true selves – that is, the harmonious will of the community.

Concerning the nature of totalitarianism, Orr contrasts two ways of theorizing about it – the syndrome way and the essentialist way. As one example of the former he takes the work of Carl Friedrich, who has developed a flexible concept of totalitarianism which now includes an all-embracing ideology, a single party typically led by one man and committed to maintaining the ideology, a highly developed system of secret police, and three forms of monopoly control – over the national economy, mass communications and operational weapons. Friedrich's syndrome theory of totalitarianism is intended to sort out actual regimes, to do justice to the complexity and shifting meaning of the concept, and to preserve the critical element of moral disapproval. It is flexible in that the features of his syndrome are not necessarily connected, nor are they intended to be exhaustive. Totalitarianism for Friedrich is a 'maturing concept'.

For Orr, the prime defect of this manner of theorizing is that in trying to keep his concept in touch with shifting usage and reality, Friedrich runs the serious risk of reducing it to hopeless ambiguity. Orr's preference appears to be for an essentialist way of theorizing which defines 'totalitarianism' exclusively in terms of one or more essential ideas. If an essentialist approach is preferred, he suggests the master-idea of a mobilized society. From this single elementary idea Orr infers some consequential components of a totalitarian state – an élitist, monopolistic party, a 'mass society', 'equality' of party and masses, the existence of 'enemies', an ideology and a centrally controlled economy. This concept of totalitarianism differs from Friedrich's syndrome in its simplicity, its exclusiveness, its universality and its neutrality.

The final essay in this collection deals with nationalism and does not require much elucidation. In the context of the sort of things we have been looking at, one would pay particular attention to Kohn's conception of nationalism, to his discussion of the burgeoning relationship during this century between nationalism and socialism, and to his use of Walt Whitman's distinction between 'open' and 'closed' forms of nationalism.

*   *   *   *

In South Africa each of the currents of political ideology covered in this work has made itself felt, some more than others. Nationalism in particular has been prominent in its various forms. Conservative and socialist, 'open' and 'closed' nationalisms have all played some role. This diversity of nationalisms suggests that a nation is not primarily a geographical area since the boundaries of nationhood are constituted rather more by an ideological delineation. What is South African and therefore what is foreign are variously interpreted. These variations are themselves not unconnected with one of the current uses of the term 'ideology', for the ideological is sometimes understood as being synonomous with what is 'foreign'. 'God preserve us from foreign ideologies', writes Chief Buthelezi in a recent newspaper article without perhaps being aware of the irony of his invocation. Another polemical use, one that is frequent in English-language newspapers, is to confine the term almost exclusively to the beliefs of Afrikaner nationalists. The National Party is portrayed as being engaged in the blind pursuit of an ideology, a pursuit that is contrasted with 'healthy, economic realism'. The belief in the rationalizing power of the market, a belief that Hayek represents, is thereby wrongly assumed not to be ideological.

As the *philosophes* of the French Enlightenment well knew, it is not easy to regard as relative one's own system of beliefs. Attitudes that prevail among groups of men always appear to them as self-evident and self-justifying. 'This all but universal illusion', writes J. S. Mill, 'is one of the examples of the magical influence of custom, which is not only, as the proverb says, a second nature, but is continually mistaken for the first'.[17]

REFERENCES

1. cf. *The Physical and Metaphysical Works of Lord Bacon*, ed. Joseph Devey (London 1891), p. 390.
2. Napoléon, *Pensées* (Paris 1913), p. 43.
3. cf. Wilhelm Reich, *The Mass Psychology of Fascism* (London 1972), ch. 1.
4. Karl Mannheim, *Ideology and Utopia* (London 1960), p. 36.
5. Ibid. p. 88, footnote 1.
6. Edward Shils, 'Ideology, the Concept and Function of Ideology' in *International Encyclopedia of the Social Sciences* (1968), Vol. 7.
7. Clifford Geertz, 'Ideology as a Cultural System', in *Ideology and Discontent* (New York 1964) edited by David Apter.
8. William T. Bluhm, *Ideologies and Attitudes: Modern Political Culture* (New Jersey 1974), p. 10.
9. John Plamenatz, *Ideology* (London 1970).
10. See p. 24.
11. See p. 44.
12. See pp. 44-45.
13. F. A. Hayek, *The Constitution of Liberty* (Chicago 1960), pp. 397-411.
14. See p. 59.
15. See p. 83.
16. See p. 121.
17. John Stuart Mill, *On Liberty*, ch. 1.

Conservatism

MICHAEL JOSEPH OAKESHOTT

Michael Oakeshott was born in Kent in 1901. He held the Chair of Political Science at the London School of Economics.

His publications include: *Experience and its Modes*, 1933; *The Social and Political Doctrines of Contemporary Europe*, 1939; *Leviathan* (ed. and intro.) 1946; *Rationalism in Politics*, 1962; *On Human Conduct*, 1975.

On being Conservative

Michael Oakeshott

The common belief that it is impossible (or, if not impossible, then so unpromising as to be not worth while attempting) to elicit explanatory general principles from what is recognized to be conservative conduct is not one that I share. It may be true that conservative conduct does not readily provoke articulation in the idiom of general ideas, and that consequently there has been a certain reluctance to undertake this kind of elucidation; but it is not to be presumed that conservative conduct is less eligible than any other for this sort or interpretation, for what it is worth. Nevertheless, this is not the enterprise I propose to engage in here. My theme is not a creed or a doctrine, but a disposition. To be conservative is to be disposed to think and behave in certain manners; it is to prefer certain kinds of conduct and certain conditions of human circumstances to others; it is to be disposed to make certain kinds of choices. And my design here is to construe this disposition as it appears in contemporary character, rather than to transpose it into the idiom of general principles.

The general characteristics of this disposition are not difficult to discern, although they have often been mistaken. They centre upon a propensity to use and to enjoy what is available rather than to wish for or to look for something else; to delight in what is present rather than what was or what may be. Reflection may bring to light an appropriate gratefulness for what is available, and consequently the acknowledgement of a gift or an inheritance from the past; but there is no mere idolizing of what is past and gone. What is esteemed is the present; and it is esteemed not on account of its connections with a remote antiquity, nor because it is recognized to be more admirable than any possible alternative, but on account of its familiarity: not, *Verweile doch, du bist so schön*, but, *Stay with me because I am attached to you.*

23

If the present is arid, offering little or nothing to be used or enjoyed, then this inclination will be weak or absent; if the present is remarkably unsettled, it will display itself in a search for a firmer foothold and consequently in a recourse to and an exploration of the past; but it asserts itself characteristically when there is much to be enjoyed, and it will be strongest when this is combined with evident risk of loss. In short, it is a disposition appropriate to a man who is acutely aware of having something to lose which he has learned to care for; a man in some degree rich in opportunities for enjoyment, but not so rich that he can afford to be indifferent to loss. It will appear more naturally in the old than in the young, not because the old are more sensitive to loss but because they are apt to be more fully aware of the resources of their world and therefore less likely to find them inadequate. In some people this disposition is weak merely because they are ignorant of what their world has to offer them: the present appears to them only as a residue of inopportunities.

To be conservative, then, is to prefer the familiar to the unknown, to prefer the tried to the untried, fact to mystery, the actual to the possible, the limited to the unbounded, the near to the distant, the sufficient to the superabundant, the convenient to the perfect, present laughter to utopian bliss. Familiar relationships and loyalties will be preferred to the allure of more profitable attachments; to acquire and to enlarge will be less important than to keep, to cultivate and to enjoy; the grief of loss will be more acute than the excitement of novelty or promise. It is to be equal to one's own fortune, to live at the level of one's own means, to be content with the want of greater perfection which belongs alike to oneself and one's circumstances. With some people this is itself a choice; in others it is a disposition which appears, frequently or less frequently, in their preferences and aversions, and is not itself chosen or specifically cultivated.

Now, all this is represented in a certain attitude towards change and innovation; change denoting alterations we have to suffer and innovation those we design and execute.

Changes are circumstances to which we have to accommodate ourselves, and the disposition to be conservative is both the emblem of our difficulty in doing so and our resort in the attempts we make to do so. Changes are without effect only upon those who notice nothing, who are ignorant of what they possess and apathetic to their circumstances; and they can be welcomed indiscriminately only by those who esteem nothing, whose attachments are fleeting and who are strangers to love and affection. The conservative disposition provokes neither of these conditions: the inclination to enjoy what is present and available is the opposite of ignorance and apathy and it breeds attachment and affection. Consequently, it is averse from change, which appears always, in the first place, as deprivation. A storm which sweeps away a copse and transforms a favourite view, the death of friends, the sleep of friendship, the desuetude of customs of behaviour, the retirement of a favourite clown, involuntary exile, reversals of fortune, the loss of abilities enjoyed and their replacement by others – these are changes, none perhaps without its compensations, which the man of conservative temperament unavoidably regrets. But he has difficulty in reconciling himself to them, not because what he has lost in them was intrinsically better than any alternative might have been or was incapable of improvement, nor because what takes its place is inherently incapable of being enjoyed, but because what he has lost was something he actually enjoyed and had learned how to enjoy and what takes its place is something to which he has acquired no attachment. Consequently, he will find small and slow changes more tolerable than large and sudden; and he will value highly every appearance of continuity. Some changes, indeed, will present no difficulty; but, again, this is not because they are manifest improvements but merely because they are easily assimilated: the changes of the seasons are mediated by their recurrence and the growing up of children by its continuousness. And, in general, he will accommodate himself more readily to changes which do not offend expectation than to the destruction of what seems to have no ground of dissolution within itself.

Moreover, to be conservative is not merely to be averse from change (which may be an idiosyncrasy); it is also a manner of accommodating ourselves to changes, an activity imposed upon all men. For change is a threat to identity, and every change is an emblem of extinction. But a man's identity (or that of a community) is nothing more than an unbroken rehearsal of contingencies, each at the mercy of circumstance and each significant in proportion to its familiarity. It is not a fortress into which we may retire, and the only means we have of defending it (that is, ourselves) against the hostile forces of change is in the open field of our experience; by throwing our weight upon the foot which for the time being is most firmly placed, by cleaving to whatever familiarities are not immediately threatened and thus assimilating what is new without becoming unrecognizable to ourselves. The Masai, when they were moved from their old country to the present Masai reserve in Kenya, took with them the names of their hills and plains and rivers and gave them to the hills and plains and rivers of the new country. And it is by some such subterfuge of conservatism that every man or people compelled to suffer a notable change avoids the shame of extinction.

Changes, then, have to be suffered; and a man of conservative temperament (that is, one strongly disposed to preserve his identity) cannot be indifferent to them. In the main, he judges them by the disturbance they entail and, like everyone else, deploys his resources to meet them. The idea of innovation, on the other hand, is improvement. Nevertheless, a man of this temperament will not himself be an ardent innovator. In the first place, he is not inclined to think that nothing is happening unless great changes are afoot and therefore he is not worried by the absence of innovation: the use and enjoyment of things as they are occupies most of his attention. Further, he is aware that not all innovation is, in fact, improvement; and he will think that to innovate without improving is either designed or inadvertent folly. Moreover, even when an innovation commends itself as a convincing improvement, he will look twice at its claims before accepting them. From his point of view, because every improvement involves change, the disruption entailed has always to be set against the benefit anticipated. But when he has satisfied himself about this, there will be other considerations to be taken into the account. Innovating is always an equivocal enterprise, in which gain and loss (even excluding the loss of familiarity) are so closely interwoven that it is exceedingly difficult to forecast the final up-shot: there is no such thing as an unqualified improvement. For innovating is an activity which generates not only the "improvement" sought, but a new and complex situation of which this is only one of the components. The total change is always more extensive than the change designed; and the whole of what is entailed can neither be foreseen nor circumscribed. Thus, whenever there is innovation there is the certainty that the change will be greater than was intended, that there will be loss as well as gain and that the loss and the gain will not be equally distributed among the people affected; there is the chance that the benefits derived will be greater than those which were designed; and there is the risk that they will be off-set by changes for the worse.

From all this the man of conservative temperament draws some appropriate conclusions. First, innovation entails certain loss and possible gain; therefore, the onus of proof, to show that the proposed change may be expected to be on the whole beneficial, rests with the would-be innovator. Secondly, he believes that the more closely an innovation resembles growth (that is, the more clearly it is intimated in and not merely imposed upon the situation) the less likely it is to result in a preponderance of loss. Thirdly, he thinks that an innovation which is a response to some specific defect, one designed to redress some specific disequilibrium, is more desirable than one which springs from a notion of a generally improved condition of human circumstances, and is far more desirable than one generated by a vision of perfection. Consequently, he prefers small and limited innovations to large and indefinite. Fourthly, he favours a slow rather than a rapid pace, and pauses to observe current consequences and make appropriate adjustments. And lastly, he believes the occasion to be important; and, other things being equal, he considers the most favourable occasion for innovation to be when the projected change is most likely to be limited to what is intended and least likely to be corrupted by undesired and unmanageable consequences.

The disposition to be conservative is, then, warm and positive in respect of enjoyment, and correspondingly cool and critical in respect of change and innovation: these two inclinations support and elucidate one another. The man of conservative temperament believes that a known good is not lightly to be surrendered for an unknown better. He is not in love with what is dangerous and difficult; he is unadventurous; he has no impulse to sail uncharted seas; for him there is no magic in being lost, bewildered or shipwrecked. If he is forced to navigate the unknown, he sees virtue in heaving the lead every inch of the way. What others plausibly identify as timidity, he recognizes in himself as rational prudence; what others interpret as inactivity, he recognizes as a disposition to enjoy rather than to exploit. He is cautious, and he is disposed to indicate his assent or dissent, not in absolute, but in graduated terms. He eyes the situation in terms of its propensity to disrupt the familiarity of the features of his world.

II

It is commonly believed that this conservative disposition is pretty deeply rooted in what is called 'human nature'. Change is tiring, innovation calls for effort, and human beings (it is said) are more apt to be lazy than energetic. If they have found a not unsatisfactory way of getting along in the world, they are not disposed to go looking for trouble. They are naturally apprehensive of the unknown and prefer safety to danger. They are reluctant innovators, and they accept change not because they like it but (as Rochefoucauld says they accept death) because it is inescapable. Change generates sadness rather than exhilaration: heaven is the dream of a changeless no less than of a perfect world. Of course, those who read 'human nature' in this way agree that this disposition does not stand alone; they merely contend that it is an exceedingly strong, perhaps the strongest, of human propensities. And, so far as it goes, there is something to be said for this belief: human circumstances would certainly be very different from what they are if there were not a large ingredient of conservatism in human preferences. Primitive peoples are said to cling to what is familiar and to be averse from change; ancient myth is full of warnings against innovation; our folklore and proverbial wisdom about the conduct of life abounds in conservative precepts; and how many tears are shed by children in their unwilling accommodation to change. Indeed, wherever a firm identity has been achieved, and wherever identity is felt to be precariously balanced, a conservative disposition is likely to prevail. On the other hand, the disposition of adolescence is often predominantly adventurous and experimental: when we are young, nothing seems more desirable than to take a chance; *pas de risque, pas de plaisir.* And while some peoples, over long stretches of time, appear successfully to have avoided change, the history of others displays periods of intense and intrepid innovation. There is, indeed, not much profit to be had from general speculation about 'human nature', which is no steadier than anything else in our acquaintance. What is more to the point is to consider current human nature, to consider ourselves.

With us, I think, the disposition to be conservative is far from being notably strong. Indeed, if he were to judge by our conduct during the last five centuries or so, an unprejudiced stranger might plausibly suppose us to be in love with change, to have an appetite only for innovation and to be either so out of sympathy with ourselves or so careless of our identity as not to be disposed to give it any consideration. In general, the fascination of what is new is felt far more keenly than the comfort of what is familiar. We are disposed to think that nothing important is happening unless great innovations are afoot, and that what is not being improved must be deteriorating. There is a positive prejudice in favour of the yet untried. We readily presume that all change is, somehow, for the better, and we are easily persuaded that all the consequences of our innovating activity are either themselves improvements or at least a reasonable price to pay for getting what we want. While the conservative, if he were forced to gamble, would bet on the field, we are disposed to back our individual fancies with little calculation and no apprehension of loss. We are acquisitive to the point of greed; ready to drop the bone we have for its reflection magnified in the mirror of the future. Nothing is made to outlast probable improvement in a world where everything is undergoing incessant improvement: the expectation of life of everything except human beings themselves continuously declines. Pieties are fleeting, loyalties evanescent, and the pace of change warns us against too deep attachments. We are willing to try anything once, regardless of the consequences. One activity vies with another in being 'up-to-date': discarded motor-cars and television sets have their counterparts in discarded moral and religious beliefs: the eye is ever on the new model. To see is to imagine what might be in the place of what is; to touch is to transform. Whatever the shape or quality of the world, it is not for long as we want it. And those in the van of movement infect those behind with their energy and enterprise. *Omnes eodem cogemur:* when we are no longer light-footed we find a place for ourselves in the band ('Which of us,' asks a contemporary, not without some equivocation, 'would not settle, at whatever cost in nervous anxiety, for a febrile and creative rather than a static society?').

Of course, our character has other ingredients besides this lust for change (we are not devoid of the impulse to cherish and preserve), but there can be little doubt about its pre-eminence. And, in these circumstances, it seems appropriate that a conservative disposition should appear, not as an intelligible (or even plausible) alternative to our mainly 'progressive' habit of mind, but either as an unfortunate hindrance to the movement afoot, or as the custodian of the museum in which quaint examples of superseded achievement are preserved for children to gape at, and as the guardian of what from time to time is considered not yet ripe for destruction, which we call (ironically enough) the amenities of life.

Here our account of the disposition to be conservative and its current fortunes might be expected to end, with the man in whom this disposition is strong last seen swimming against the tide, disregarded not because what he has to say is necessarily false but because it has become irrelevant; outmanoeuvred, not on account of any intrinsic demerit but merely by the flow of circumstance; a faded, timid, nostalgic character, provoking pity as an outcast and contempt as a reactionary. Nevertheless, I think there is something more to be said. Even in these circumstances, when a conservative disposition in respect of things in general is unmistakably at a discount, there are occasions when this disposition remains not only appropriate, but supremely so; and there are connections in which we are unavoidably disposed in a conservative direction.

In the first place, there is a certain kind of activity (not yet extinct) which can be engaged in only in virtue of a disposition to be conservative, namely, activities where what is sought is present enjoyment and not a profit, a reward, a prize or a result in addition to the experience itself. And when these activities are recognized as the emblems of this disposition, to be conservative is disclosed, not as prejudiced hostility to a 'progressive' attitude capable of embracing the whole range of human conduct, but as a disposition exclusively appropriate in a large and significant field of human activity. And the man in whom this disposition is pre-eminent appears as one who prefers to engage in activities where to be conservative is uniquely appropriate, and not as a man inclined to impose his conservatism indiscriminately upon all human activity. In short, if we find ourselves (as most of us do) inclined to reject conservatism as a disposition appropriate in respect of human conduct in general, there still remains a certain kind of human conduct for which this disposition is not merely appropriate but a necessary condition.

There are, of course, numerous human relationships in which a disposition to be conservative, a disposition merely to enjoy what they offer for its own sake, is not particularly appropriate: master and servant, owner and bailiff, buyer and seller, principal and agent. In these, each participant seeks some service or some recompense for service. A customer who finds a shopkeeper unable to supply his wants either persuades him to enlarge his stock or goes elsewhere; and a shopkeeper unable to meet the desires of a customer tries to impose upon him others which he can satisfy. A principal ill-served by his agent, looks for another. A servant ill-recompensed for his service, asks for a rise; and one dissatisfied with his conditions of work, seeks a change. In short, these are all relationships in which some result is sought; each party is concerned with the ability of the other to provide it. If what is sought is lacking, it is to be expected that the relationship will lapse or be terminated. To be conservative in such relationships, to enjoy what is present and available regardless of its failure to satisfy any want and merely because it has struck our fancy and become familiar, is conduct which discloses a *jusqu' auboutiste* conservatism, an irrational inclination to refuse all relationships which call for the exercise of any other disposition. Though even these relationships seem to lack something appropriate to them when they are confined to a nexus of supply and demand and allow no room for the intrusion of the loyalties and attachments which spring from familiarity.

But there are relationships of another kind in which no result is sought and which are engaged in for their own sake and enjoyed for what they are and not for what they provide. This is so of friendship. Here, attachment springs from an intimation of familiarity and subsists in a mutual sharing of personalities. To go on changing one's butcher until one gets the meat one likes, to go on educating one's agent until he does what is required of him, is conduct not inappropriate to the relationship concerned; but to discard friends because they do not behave as we expected and refuse to be educated to our requirements is the conduct of a man who has altogether mistaken the character of friendship. Friends are not concerned with what might be made of one another, but only with the enjoyment of one another; and the condition of this enjoyment is a ready acceptance of what is and the absence of any desire to change or to improve. A friend is not somebody one trusts to behave in a certain manner, who supplies certain wants, who has certain useful abilities, who possesses certain merely agreeable qualities, or who holds certain acceptable opinions; he is somebody who engages the imagination, who excites contemplation, who provokes interest, sympathy, delight and loyalty simply on account of the relationship entered into. One friend cannot replace another; there is all the difference in the world between the death of a friend and the retirement of one's tailor from business. The relationship of friend to friend is dramatic, not utilitarian; the tie is one of familiarity, not usefulness; the disposition engaged is conservative, not 'progressive'. And what is true of friendship is not less true of other experiences – of patriotism, for example, and of conversation – each of which demands a conservative disposition as a condition of its enjoyment.

But further, there are activities, not involving human relationships, that may be engaged in, not for a prize, but for the enjoyment they generate, and for which the only appropriate disposition is the disposition to be conservative. Consider fishing. If your project is merely to catch fish it would be foolish to be unduly conservative. You will seek out the best tackle, you will discard practices which prove unsuccessful, you will not be bound by unprofitable attachments to particular localities, pieties will be fleeting, loyalties evanescent; you may even be wise to try anything once in the hope of improvement. But fishing is an activity that may be engaged in, not for the profit of a catch, but for its own sake; and the fisherman may return home in the evening not less content for being empty-handed. Where this is so, the activity has become a ritual and a conservative disposition is appropriate. Why worry about the best gear if you do not care whether or not you make a catch? What matters is the enjoyment of exercising skill (or, perhaps, merely passing the time),[1] and this is to be had with any tackle, so long as it is familiar and is not grotesquely inappropriate.

All activities, then, where what is sought is enjoyment springing, not from the success of the enterprise but from the familiarity of the engagement, are emblems of the disposition to be conservative. And there are many of them. Fox placed gambling among them when he said that it gave two supreme pleasures, the pleasure of winning and the pleasure of losing. Indeed, I can think of only one activity of this kind which seems to call for a disposition other than conservative: the love of fashion, that is, wanton delight in change for its own sake no matter what it generates.

But, besides the not inconsiderable class of activities which we can engage in only in virtue of a disposition to be conservative, there are occasions in the conduct of other activities when this is the most appropriate disposition; indeed there are few activities which do not, at some point or other, make a call upon it. Whenever stability is more profitable than improvement, whenever certainty is more valuable than speculation, whenever familiarity is more desirable than perfection, whenever agreed error is superior to controversial truth, whenever the disease is more sufferable than the cure, whenever the satisfaction of expectations is more important than the 'justice' of the expectations themselves, whenever a rule of some sort is better than the risk of having no rule at all, a disposition to be conservative will be more appropriate than any other; and on any reading of human conduct these cover a not negligible range of circumstances. Those who see the man of conservative disposition (even in what is vulgarly called a 'progressive' society) as a lonely swimmer battling against the overwhelming current of circumstance must be thought to have adjusted their binoculars to exclude a large field of human occasion.

In most activities not engaged in for their own sake a distinction appears, at a certain level of observation, between the project undertaken and the means employed, between the enterprise and the tools used for its achievement. This is not, of course, an absolute distinction; projects are often provoked and governed by the tools available, and on rarer occasions the tools are designed to fit a particular project. And what on one occasion is a project, on another is a tool. Moreover there is at least one significant exception: the activity of being a poet. It is, however, a relative distinction of some usefulness because it calls our attention to an appropriate difference of attitude towards the two components of the situation.

In general, it may be said that our disposition in respect of tools is appropriately more conservative than our attitude towards projects; or, in other words, tools are less subject to innovation than projects because, except on rare occasions, tools are not designed to fit a particular project and th⸳⸳ chrown aside, they are designed to fit a whole class of projects. And this is intelligible because most tools call for skill in use and skill is inseparable from practice and familiarity: a skilled man, whether he is a sailor, a cook or an accountant, is a man familiar with a certain stock of tools. Indeed, a carpenter is usually more skilful in handling his own tools than in handling other examples of the kind of tools commonly used by carpenters; and the solicitor can use his own (annotated) copy of Pollock on *Partnership* or Jarman on *Wills* more readily than any other. Familiarity is the essence of tool using; and in so far as man is a tool using animal he is disposed to be conservative.

Many of the tools in common use have remained unchanged for generations; the design of others has undergone considerable modification; and our stock of tools is always being enlarged by new inventions and improved by new designs. Kitchens, factories, workshops, building sites and offices disclose a characteristic mixture of long-tried and newly invented equipment. But, be that how it may, when business of any kind is afoot, when a particular project has been engaged in – whether it is baking a pie or shoeing a horse, floating a loan or a company, selling fish or insurance to a customer, building a ship or a suit of clothes, sowing wheat or lifting potatoes, laying down port or putting up a barrage – we recognize it to be an occasion when it is particularly appropriate to be conservative about the tools we employ. If it is a large project, we put it in the charge of a man who has the requisite knowledge, and we expect him to engage subordinates who know their own business and are skilled in the use of certain stocks of tools. At some point in this hierarchy of tool-users the suggestion may be made that in order to do this particular job an addition or modification is required in the available stock of tools. Such a suggestion is likely to come from somewhere about the middle of the hierarchy: we do not expect a designer to say 'I must go away and do some fundamental research which will take me five years before I can go on with the job' (his bag of tools is a body of knowledge and we expect him to have it handy and to know his way about it); and we do not expect the man at the bottom to have a stock of tools in-adequate for the needs of his particular part. But even if such a suggestion is made and is followed up, it will not disrupt the appropriateness of a conservative disposition in respect of the whole stock of tools being used. Indeed, it is clear enough that no job would ever get done, no piece of business could ever be transacted if, on the occasion, our disposition in respect of our tools were not, generally speaking, conservative. And since doing business of one sort or another occupies most of our time and little can be done without tools of some kind, the disposition to be conservative occupies an unavoidably large place in our character.

The carpenter comes to do a job, perhaps one the exact like of which he has never before tackled; but he comes with his bag of familiar tools and his only chance of doing the job lies in the skill with which he uses what he has at his disposal. When the plumber goes to fetch his tools he would be away even longer than is usually the case if his purpose were to invent new or to improve old ones. Nobody questions the value of money in the market place. No business would ever get done if, before a pound of cheese were weighed or a pint of beer drawn, the relative usefulness of these particular scales of weight and measurement as compared with others were thrashed out. The surgeon does not pause in the middle of an operation to redesign his instruments. The MCC does not authorize a new width of bat, a new weight of ball or a new length of wicket in the middle of a Test Match, or even in the middle of a cricket season. When your house is on fire you do not get in touch with a fire-prevention research station to design a new appliance; as Disraeli pointed out, unless you are a lunatic, you send for the parish fire-engine. A musician may improvise music, but he would think himself hardly done-by if, at the same time, he were expected to improvise an instrument. Indeed, when a particularly tricky job is to be done, the workman will often prefer to use a tool that he is thoroughly familiar with rather than another he has in his bag, of new design, but which he has not yet mastered the use of. No doubt there is a time and a place to be radical about such things, for promoting innovation and carrying out improvements in the tools we employ, but these are clearly occasions for the exercise of a conservative disposition.

Now, what is true about tools in general, as distinct from projects, is even more obviously true about a certain kind of tool in common use, namely, general rules of conduct. If the familiarity that springs from relative immunity from change is appropriate to hammers and pincers and to bats and balls, it is supremely appropriate, for example, to an office routine. Routines, no doubt, are susceptible of improvement; but the more familiar they become, the more useful they are. Not to have a conservative disposition in respect of a routine is obvious folly. Of course, exceptional occasions occur which may call for a dispensation; but an inclination to be conservative rather than reformist about a routine is unquestionably appropriate. Consider the conduct of a public meeting, the rules of debate in the House of Commons or the procedure of a court of law. The chief virtue of these arrangements is that they are fixed and familiar; they establish and satisfy certain expectations, they allow to be said in a convenient order whatever is relevant, they prevent extraneous collisions and they conserve human energy. They are typical tools – instruments eligible for use in a variety of different but similar jobs. They are the product of reflection and choice, there is nothing sacrosanct about them, they are susceptible of change and improvement; but if our disposition in respect of them were not, generally speaking, conservative, if we were disposed to argue about them and change them on every occasion, they would rapidly lose their value. And while there may be rare occasions when it is useful to suspend them, it is pre-eminently appropriate that they should not be innovated upon or improved while they are in operation. Or again, consider the rules of a game. These, also, are the product of reflection and choice, and there are occasions when it is appropriate to reconsider them in the light of current experience; but it is inappropriate to have anything but a conservative disposition towards them or to consider putting them all together at one time into the melting-pot; and it is supremely inappropriate to change or improve upon them in the heat and confusion of play. Indeed, the more eager each side is to win, the more valuable is an inflexible set of rules. Players in the course of play may devise new tactics, they may improvise new methods of attack and defence, they may do anything they choose to defeat the expectations of their opponents, except invent new rules. That is an activity to be indulged sparingly and then only in the off-season.

There is much more that might be said about the relevance of the disposition to be conservative and its appropriateness even in a character, such as ours, chiefly disposed in the opposite direction. I have said nothing of morals, nothing of religion; but perhaps I have said enough to show that, even if to be conservative on all occasions and in all connections is so remote from our habit of thought as to be almost unintelligible, there are, nevertheless, few of our activities which do not on all occasions call into partnership a disposition to be conservative and on some occasions recognize it as the senior partner; and there are some activities where it is properly master.

III

How, then, are we to construe the disposition to be conservative in respect of politics? And in making this inquiry what I am interested in is not merely the intelligibility of this disposition in any set of circumstances, but its intelligibility in our own contemporary circumstances.

Writers who have considered this question commonly direct our attention to beliefs about the world in general, about human beings in general, about associations in general and even about the universe; and they tell us that a conservative disposition in politics can be correctly construed only when we understand it as a reflection of certain beliefs of these kinds. It is said, for example, that conservatism in politics is the appropriate counterpart of a generally conservative disposition in respect of human conduct: to be reformist in business, in morals or in religion and to be conservative in politics is represented as being inconsistent. It is said that the conservative in politics is so by virtue of holding certain religious beliefs; a belief, for example, in a natural law to be gathered from human experience, and in a providential order reflecting a divine purpose in nature and in human history to which it is the duty of mankind to conform its conduct and departure from which spells injustice and calamity. Further, it is said that a disposition to be conservative in politics reflects what is called an 'organic' theory of human society; that it is tied up with a belief in the absolute value of human personality, and with a belief in a primordial propensity of human beings to sin. And the 'conservatism' of an Englishman has even been connected with Royalism and Anglicanism.

Now, setting aside the minor complaints one might be moved to make about this account of the situation, it seems to me to suffer from one large defect. It is true that many of these beliefs have been held by people disposed to be conservative in political activity, and it may be true that these people have also believed their disposition to be in some way confirmed by them, or even to be founded upon them; but, as I understand it, a disposition to be conservative in politics does not entail either that we should hold these beliefs to be true or even that we should suppose them to be true. Indeed, I do not think it is necessarily connected with any particular beliefs about the universe, about the world in general or about human conduct in general. What it is tied to is certain beliefs about the activity of governing and the instruments of government, and it is in terms of beliefs on these topics, and not on others, that it can be made to appear intelligible. And, to state my view briefly before elaborating it, what makes a conservative disposition in politics intelligible is nothing to do with a natural law or a providential order, nothing to do with morals or religion; it is the observation of our current manner of living combined with the belief (which from our point of view need be regarded as no more than an hypothesis) that governing is a specific and limited activity, namely the provision and custody of general rules of conduct, which are understood, not as plans for imposing substantive activities, but as instruments enabling people to pursue the activities of their own choice with the minimum frustration, and therefore something which it is appropriate to be conservative about.

Let us begin at what I believe to be the proper starting-place; not in the empyrean, but with ourselves as we have come to be. I and my neighbours, my associates, my compatriots, my friends, my enemies and those who I am indifferent about, are people engaged in a great variety of activities. We are apt to entertain a multiplicity of opinions on every conceivable subject and are disposed to change these beliefs as we grow tired of them or as they prove unserviceable. Each of us is pursuing a course of his own; and there is no project so unlikely that somebody will not be found to engage in it, no enterprise so foolish that somebody will not undertake it. There are those who spend their lives trying to sell copies of the Anglican Catechism to the Jews. And one half of the world is engaged in trying to make the other half want what it has hitherto never felt the lack of. We are all inclined to be passionate about our own concerns, whether it is making things or selling them, whether it is business or sport, religion or learning, poetry, drink or drugs. Each of us has preferences of his own. For some, the opportunities of making choices (which are numerous) are invitations readily accepted; others welcome them less eagerly or even find them burdensome. Some dream dreams of new and better worlds: others are more inclined to move in familiar paths or even to be idle. Some are apt to deplore the rapidity of change, others delight in it; all recognize it. At times we grow tired and fall asleep: it is a blessed relief to gaze in a shop window and see nothing we want; we are grateful for ugliness merely because it repels attention. But, for the most part, we pursue happiness by seeking the satisfaction of desires which spring from one another inexhaustably. We enter into relationships of interest and of emotion, of competition, partnership, guardianship, love, friendship, jealousy and hatred, some of which are more durable than others. We make agreements with one another; we have expectations about one another's conduct; we approve, we are indifferent and we disapprove. This multiplicity of activity and variety of opinion is apt to produce collisions: we pursue courses which cut across those of others, and we do not all approve the same sort of conduct. But, in the main, we get along with one another, sometimes by giving way, sometimes by standing fast, sometimes in a compromise. Our conduct consists of activity assimilated to that of others in small, and for the most part unconsidered and unobtrusive, adjustments.

Why all this should be so, does not matter. It is not necessarily so. A different condition of human circumstance can easily be imagined, and we know that elsewhere and at other times activity is, or has been, far less multifarious and changeful and opinion far less diverse and far less likely to provoke collision, but, by and large, we recognize this to be our condition. It is an acquired condition, though nobody designed or specifically chose it in preference to all others. It is the product, not of 'human nature' let loose, but of human beings impelled by an acquired love of making choices for themselves. And we know as little and as much about where it is leading us as we know about the fashion in hats of twenty years' time or the design of motorcars.

Surveying the scene, some people are provoked by the absence of order and coherence which appears to them to be its dominant feature; its wastefulness, its frustration, its dissipation of human energy, its lack not merely of a premeditated destination but even of any discernible direction of movement. It provides an excitement similar to that of a stock-car race; but it has none of the satisfaction of a well-conducted business enterprise. Such people are apt to exaggerate the current disorder; the absence of plan is so conspicuous that the small adjustments, and even the more massive arrangements, which restrain the chaos seem to them nugatory; they have no feeling for the warmth of untidiness but only for its inconvenience. But what is significant is not the limitations of their powers of observation, but the turn of their thoughts. They feel that there ought to be something that ought to be done to convert this so-called chaos into order, for this is no way for rational human beings to be spending their lives. Like Apollo when he saw Daphne with her hair hung carelessly about her neck, they sigh and say to themselves: 'What if it were properly arranged.' Moreover, they tell us that they have seen in a dream the glorious, collisionless manner of living proper to all mankind, and this dream they understand as their warrant for seeking to remove the diversities and occasions of conflict which distinguish our current manner of living. Of course, their dreams are not all exactly alike; but they have this in common: each is a vision of a condition of human circumstance from which the occasion of conflict has been removed, a vision of human activity co-ordinated and set going in a single direction and of every resource being used to the full. And such people appropriately understand the office of government to be the imposition upon its subjects of the condition of human circumstances of their dream. To govern is to turn a private dream into a public and compulsory manner of living. Thus, politics becomes an encounter of dreams and the activity in which government is held to this understanding of its office and provided with the appropriate instruments.

I do not propose to criticize this jump to glory style of politics in which governing is understood as a perpetual take-over bid for the purchase of the resources of human energy in order to concentrate them in a single direction; it is not at all unintelligible, and there is much in our circumstances to provoke it. My purpose is merely to point out that there is another quite different understanding of government, and that it is no less intelligible and in some respects perhaps more appropriate to our circumstances.

The spring of this other disposition in respect of governing and the instruments of government – a conservative disposition – is to be found in the acceptance of the current condition of human circumstances as I have described it: the propensity to make our own choices and to find happiness in doing so, the variety of enterprises each pursued with passion, the diversity of beliefs each held with the conviction of its exclusive truth;

the inventiveness, the changefulness and the absence of any large design; the excess, the over-activity and the informal compromise. And the office of government is not to impose other beliefs and activities upon its subjects, not to tutor or to educate them, not to make them better or happier in another way, not to direct them, to galvanize them into action, to lead them or to co-ordinate their activities so that no occasion of conflict shall occur; the office of government is merely to rule. This is a specific and limited activity, easily corrupted when it is combined with any other, and, in the circumstances, indispensable. The image of the ruler is the umpire whose business is to administer the rules of the game, or the chairman who governs the debate according to known rules but does not himself participate in it.

Now people of this disposition commonly defend their belief that the proper attitude of government towards the current condition of human circumstance is one of acceptance by appealing to certain general ideas. They contend that there is absolute value in the free play of human choice, that private property (the emblem of choice) is a natural right, that it is only in the enjoyment of diversity of opinion and activity that true belief and good conduct can be expected to disclose themselves. But I do not think that this disposition requires these or any similar beliefs in order to make it intelligible. Something much smaller and less pretentious will do: the observation that this condition of human circumstance is, in fact, current, and that we have learned to enjoy it and how to manage it; that we are not children *in statu pupillari* but adults who do not consider themselves under any obligation to justify their preference for making their own choices; and that it is beyond human experience to suppose that those who rule are endowed with a superior wisdom which discloses to them a better range of beliefs and activities and which gives them authority to impose upon their subjects a quite different manner of life. In short, if the man of this disposition is asked: Why ought governments to accept the current diversity of opinion and activity in preference to imposing upon their subjects a dream of their own? it is enough for him to reply: Why not? Their dreams are no different from those of anyone else; and if it is boring to have to listen to dreams of others being recounted, it is insufferable to be forced to re-enact them. We tolerate monomaniacs, it is our habit to do so; but why should we be *ruled* by them? Is it not (the man of conservative disposition asks) an intelligible task for a government to protect its subjects against the nuisance of those who spend their energy and their wealth in the service of some pet indignation, endeavouring to impose it upon everybody, not by suppressing their activities in favour of others of a similar kind, but by setting a limit to the amount of noise anyone may emit?

Nevertheless, if this acceptance is the spring of the conservative's disposition in respect of government, he does not suppose that the office of government is to do nothing. As he understands it, there is work to be done which can be done only in virtue of a genuine acceptance of current beliefs simply because they are current and current activities simply because they are afoot. And, briefly, the office he attributes to government is to resolve some of the collisions which this variety of beliefs and activities generates; to preserve peace, not by placing an interdict upon choice and upon the diversity that springs from the exercise of preference, not by imposing substantive uniformity, but by enforcing general rules of procedure upon all subjects alike.

Government, then, as the conservative in this matter understands it, does not begin with a vision of another, different and better world, but with the observation of the self-government practised even by men of passion in the conduct of their enterprises; it begins in the informal adjustments of interests to one another which are designed to release those who are apt to collide from the mutual frustration of a collision. Sometimes these adjustments are no more than agreements between two parties to keep out of each other's way; sometimes they are of wider application and more durable character, such as the International Rules for the prevention of collisions at sea. In short, the intimations of government are to be found in ritual, not in religion or philosophy; in the enjoyment of orderly and peaceable behaviour, not in the search for truth or perfection.

But the self-government of men of passionate belief and enterprise is apt to break down when it is most needed. It often suffices to resolve minor collisions of interest, but beyond these it is not to be relied upon. A more precise and less easily corrupted ritual is required to resolve the massive collisions which our manner of living is apt to generate and to release us from the massive frustrations in which we are apt to become locked. The custodian of this ritual is 'the government', and the rules it imposes are 'the law'. One may imagine a government engaged in the activity of an arbiter in cases of collisions of interest but doing its business without the aid of laws, just as one may imagine a game without rules and an umpire who was appealed to in cases of dispute and who on each occasion merely used his judgement to devise *ad hoc* a way of realeasing the disputants from their mutual frustration. But the diseconomy of such an arrangement is so obvious that it could only be expected to occur to those inclined to believe the ruler to be supernaturally inspired and to those disposed to attribute to him a quite different office – that of leader, or tutor, or manager. At all events the disposition to be conservative in respect of government is rooted in the belief that where government rests upon the acceptance of the current activities and beliefs of its subjects, the only appropriate manner of ruling is by making and enforcing rules of conduct. In short, to be conservative about government is a reflection of the conservatism we have recognized to be appropriate in respect of rules of conduct.

To govern, then, as the conservative understands it, is to provide a *vinculum juris* for those manners of conduct which, in the circumstances, are least likely to result in a frustrating collision of interests; to provide redress and means of compensation for those who suffer from others behaving in a contrary manner; sometimes to provide punishment for those who pursue their own interests regardless of the rules; and, of course, to provide a sufficient force to maintain the authority of an arbiter of this kind. Thus, governing is recognized as a specific and limited activity; not the management of an enterprise, but the rule of those engaged in a great diversity of self-chosen enterprises. It is not concerned with concrete persons, but with activities; and with activities only in respect of their propensity to collide with one another. It is not concerned with moral right and wrong, it is not designed to make men good or even better; it is not indispensable on account of 'the natural depravity of mankind' but merely because of their current disposition to be extravagant; its business is to keep its subjects at peace with one another in the activities in which they have chosen to seek their happiness. And if there is any general idea entailed in this view, it is, perhaps, that a government which does not sustain the loyalty of its subjects is worthless; and that while one which (in the old puritan phrase) 'commands for truth' is incapable of doing so (because some of its subjects will believe its 'truth' to be error), one which is indifferent to 'truth' and 'error' alike, and merely pursues peace, presents no obstacle to the necessary loyalty.

Now, it is intelligible enough that any man who thinks in this manner about government should be averse from innovation: government is providing rules of conduct, and familiarity is a supremely important virtue in a rule. Nevertheless, he has room for other thoughts. The current condition of human circumstances is one in which new activities (often springing from new inventions) are constantly appearing and rapidly extend themselves, and in which beliefs are perpetually being modified or discarded; and for the rules to be inappropriate to the current activities and beliefs is as unprofitable as for them to be unfamiliar. For example, a variety of inventions and considerable changes in the conduct of business, seem now to have made the current law of copyright inadequate. And it may be thought that neither the newspaper nor the motor-car nor the aeroplane have yet received proper recognition in the law of England; they have all created nuisances that call out to be abated. Or again, at the end of the last century our governments engaged in an extensive codification of large parts of our law and in this manner both brought it into closer relationship with current beliefs and manners of activity and insulated it from the small adjustments to circumstances which are characteristic of the operation of our common law. But many of these Statutes are now hopelessly out of date. And there are older Acts of Parliament (such as the Merchant Shipping Act), governing large and important departments of activity, which are even more inappropriate to current circumstances. Innovation, then, is called for if the rules are to remain appropriate to the activities they govern. But, as the conservative understands it, modification of the rules should always reflect, and never impose, a change in the activities and beliefs of those who are subject to them, and should never on any occasion be so great as to destroy the ensemble. Consequently, the conservative will have nothing to do with innovations designed to meet merely hypothetical situations; he will prefer to enforce a rule he has got rather than invent a new one; he will think it appropriate to delay a modification of the rules until it is clear that the change of circumstance it is designed to reflect has come to stay for a while; he will be suspicious of proposals for change in excess of what the situation calls for, of rulers who demand extra-ordinary powers in order to make great changes and whose utterances are tied to generalities like 'the public good' or 'social justice', and of Saviours of Society who buckle on armour and seek dragons to slay; he will think it proper to consider the occasion of the innovation with care; in short, he will be disposed to regard politics as an activity in which a valuable set of tools is renovated from time to time and kept in trim rather than as an opportunity for perpetual re-equipment.

All this may help to make intelligible the disposition to be conservative in respect of government; and the detail might be elaborated to show, for example, how a man of this disposition understands the other great business of a government, the con-duct of a foreign policy; to show why he places so high a value upon the complicated set of arrangements we call 'the institu-tion of private property'; to show the appropriateness of his rejection of the view that politics is a shadow thrown by econo-mics; to show why he believes that the main (perhaps the only) specifically economic activity appropriate to government is the maintenance of a stable currency. But, on this occasion, I think there is something else to be said.

To some people, 'government' appears as a vast reservoir of power which inspires them to dream of what use might be made of it. They have favourite projects, of various dimensions, which they sincerely believe are for the benefit of mankind, and to capture this source of power, if necessary to increase it, and to use it for imposing their favourite projects upon their fellows is what they understand as the adventure of governing men. They are, thus, disposed to recognize government as an instrument of passion; the art of politics is to inflame and direct desire. In short, governing is understood to be just like any other activity – making and selling a brand of soap, exploiting the resources of a locality, or developing a housing estate – only the power here is (for the most part) already mobilized, and the enterprise is remarkable only because it aims at monopoly and because of its promise of success once the source of power has been captured. Of course a private enterprise politician of this sort would get nowhere in these days unless there were people with wants so vague that they can be prompted to ask for what he has to offer, or with wants so servile that they prefer the promise of a provided abundance to the opportunity of choice and activity on their own account. And it is not all as plain sailing as it might appear: often a politician of this sort misjudges the situation; and then, briefly, even in democratic politics, we become aware of what the camel thinks of the camel driver.

Now, the disposition to be conservative in respect of politics reflects a quite different view of the activity of governing. The man of this disposition understands it to be the business of a government not to inflame passion and give it new objects to feed upon, but to inject into the activities of already too passionate men an ingredient of moderation; to restrain, to deflate, to pacify and to reconcile; not to stoke the fires of desire, but to damp them down. And all this, not because passion is vice and moderation virtue, but because moderation is indispensable if passionate men are to escape being locked in an encounter of mutual frustration. A government of this sort does not need to be regarded as the agent of a benign providence, as the custodian of a moral law, or as the emblem of a divine order. What it provides is something that its subjects (if they are such people as we are) can easily recognize to be valuable; indeed, it is something that, to some extent, they do for themselves in the ordinary course of business or pleasure. They scarcely need to be reminded of its indispensability, as Sextus Empiricus tells us the ancient Persians were accustomed periodically to remind themselves by setting aside all laws for five hair-raising days on the death of a king. Generally speaking, they are not averse from paying the modest cost of this service; and they recognize that the appropriate attitude to a government of this sort is loyalty (sometimes a confident loyalty, at others perhaps the heavy-hearted loyalty of Sidney Godolphin), respect and some suspicion, not love or devotion or affection. Thus, governing is understood to be a secondary activity; but it is recognized also to be a specific activity, not easily to be combined with any other, because all other activities (except the mere contemplation of the scene) entail taking sides and the surrender of the indifference appropriate (on this view of things) not only to the judge but also to the legislator, who is understood to occupy a judicial office. The subjects of such a government require that it shall be strong, alert, resolute, economical and neither capricious nor over-active: they have no use for a referee who does not govern the game according to the rules, who takes sides, who plays a game of his own, or who is always blowing his whistle; after all, the game's the thing, and in playing the game we neither need to be, nor at present are disposed to be, conservative.

But there is something more to be observed in this style of governing than merely the restraint imposed by familiar and appropriate rules. Of course, it will not countenance government by suggestion or cajolery or by any other means than by law; an avuncular Home Secretary or a threatening Chancellor of the Exchequer. But the spectacle of its indifference to the beliefs and substantive activities of its subjects may itself be expected to provoke a habit of restraint. Into the heat of our engagements, into the passionate clash of beliefs, into our enthusiasm for saving the souls of our neighbours or of all mankind, a government of this sort injects an ingredient, not of reason (how should we expect that?) but of the irony that is prepared to counteract one vice by another, of the raillery that deflates extravagance without itself pretending to wisdom, of the mockery that disperses tension, of inertia and of scepticism: indeed, it might be said that we keep a government of this sort to do for us the scepticism we have neither the time nor the inclination to do for ourselves. It is like the cool touch of the mountain that one feels in the plain even on the hottest summer day. Or, to leave metaphor behind, it is like the 'governor' which, by controlling the speed at which its parts move, keeps an engine from racketing itself to pieces.

It is not, then, mere stupid prejudice which disposes a conservative to take this view of the activity of governing; nor are any highfalutin metaphysical beliefs necessary to provoke it or make it intelligible. It is connected merely with the observation that where activity is bent upon enterprise the indispensable counterpart is another order of activity, bent upon restraint, which is unavoidably corrupted (indeed, altogether abrogated) when the power assigned to it is used for advancing favourite projects. An 'umpire' who at the same time is one of the players is no umpire; 'rules' about which we are not disposed to be conservative are not rules but incitements to disorder; the conjunction of dreaming and ruling generates tyranny.

IV

Political conservatism is, then, not at all unintelligible in a people disposed to be adventurous and enterprising, a people in love with change and apt to rationalize their affections in terms of 'progress'. (I have not forgotten to ask myself the question: Why, then, have we so neglected what is appropriate to our circumstances as to make the activist dreamer the stereotype of the modern politician? And I have tried to answer it elsewhere.) And one does not need to think that the belief in 'progress' is the most cruel and unprofitable of all beliefs, arousing cupidity without satisfying it, in order to think it inappropriate for a government to be conspicuously 'progressive'. Indeed, a disposition to be conservative in respect of government would seem to be pre-eminently appropriate to men who have something to do and something to think about on their own account, who have a skill to practise or an intellectual fortune to make, to people whose passions do not need to be inflamed, whose desires do not need to be provoked and whose dreams of a better world need no prompting. Such people know the value of a rule which imposes orderliness without directing enterprise, a rule which concentrates duty so that room is left for delight. They might even be prepared to suffer a legally established ecclesiastical order; but it would not be because they believed it to represent some unassailable religious truth, but merely because it restrained the indecent competition of sects and (as Hume said) moderated 'the plague of a too diligent clergy'.

Now, whether or not these beliefs recommend themselves as reasonable and appropriate to our circumstances and to the abilities we are likely to find in those who rule us, they and their like are in my view what make intelligible a conservative disposition in respect of politics. What would be the appropriateness of this disposition in circumstances other than our own, whether to be conservative in respect of government would have the same relevance in the circumstances of an unadventurous, a slothful or a spiritless people, is a question we need not try to answer: we are concerned with ourselves as we are. I myself think that it would occupy an important place in any set of circumstances But what I hope I have made clear is that it is not at all inconsistent to be conservative in respect of government and radical in respect of almost every other activity And, in my opinion, there is more to be learnt about this disposition from Montaigne, Pascal, Hobbes and Hume than from Burke or Bentham.

Of the many entailments of this view of things that might be pointed to, I will notice one, namely, that politics is an activity unsuited to the young, not on account of their vices but on account of what I at least consider to be their virtues.

Nobody pretends that it is easy to acquire or to sustain the mood of indifference which this manner of politics calls for. To rein-in one's own beliefs and desires, to acknowledge the current shape of things, to feel the balance of things in one's hand, to tolerate what is abominable, to distinguish between crime and sin, to respect formality even when it appears to be leading to error, these are difficult achievements; and they are achievements not to be looked for in the young.

Everybody's young days are a dream, a delightful insanity, a sweet solipsism. Nothing in them has a fixed shape, nothing a fixed price; everything is a possibility, and we live happily on credit. There are no obligations to be observed; there are no accounts to be kept. Nothing is specified in advance; everything is what can be made of it. The world is a mirror in which we seek the reflection of our own desires. The allure of violent emotions is irresistible. When we are young we are not disposed to make concessions to the world; we never feel the balance of a thing in our hands – unless it be a cricket bat. We are not apt to distinguish between our liking and our esteem; urgency is our criterion of importance; and we do not easily understand that what is humdrum need not be despicable. We are impatient of restraint; and we readily believe, like Shelley, that to have contracted a habit is to have failed. These, in my opinion, are among our virtues when we are young; but how remote they are from the disposition appropriate for participating in the style of government I have been describing. Since life is a dream, we argue (with plausible but erroneous logic) that politics must be an encounter of dreams, in which we hope to impose our own. Some unfortunate people, like Pitt (laughably called 'the Younger'), are born old, and are eligible to engage in politics almost in their cradles; others, perhaps more fortunate, belie the saying that one is young only once, they never grow up. But these are exceptions. For most there is what Conrad called the 'shadow line' which, when we pass it, discloses a solid world of things, each with its fixed shape, each with its own point of balance, each with its price; a world of fact, not poetic image, in which what we have spent on one thing we cannot spend on another; a world inhabited by others besides ourselves who cannot be reduced to mere reflections of our own emotions. And coming to be at home in this commonplace world qualifies us (as no knowledge of 'political science' can ever qualify us), if we are so inclined and have nothing better to think about, to engage in what the man of conservative disposition understands to be political activity.

REFERENCE

1. When Prince Wen Wang was on a tour of inspection in Tsang, he saw an old man fishing. But his fishing was not real fishing, for he did not fish in order to catch fish, but to amuse himself. So Wen Wang wished to employ him in the administration of government, but he feared his own ministers, uncles and brothers might object. On the other hand, if he let the old man go, he could not bear to think of the people being deprived of his influence. *Chuang Tzu.*

Liberalism

FRIEDRICH AUGUST HAYEK

Friedrich Hayek was born in Vienna in 1899. He was director of the Austrian Institute of Economic Research before moving to England in 1931. In 1950 he was Professor of Social and Moral Science at the University of Chicago. In 1962 he was appointed Professor of Economics at the University of Freiburg. He was awarded the 1974 Nobel Prize for Economics.

His publications include: *The Road to Serfdom*, 1944; *Individualism and Economic Order*, 1949; *John Stuart Mill and Harriet Taylor*, 1951; *The Counter-Revolution of Science*, 1952; *Capitalism and the Historians* (ed.) 1954; *The Political Ideal of the Rule of Law*, 1955; *The Constitution of Liberty*, 1960; *Studies in Philosophy, Politics and Economics*, 1967; *The Confusion of Language in Political Thought*, 1968; *Freiburger Studies*, 1969.

The Principles of a Liberal Social Order

F. A. Hayek

By 'liberalism' I shall understand here the conception of a desirable political order which in the first instance was developed in England from the time of the Old Whigs in the later part of the seventeenth century to that of Gladstone at the end of the nineteenth. David Hume, Adam Smith, Edmund Burke, T. B. Macaulay and Lord Acton may be regarded as its typical representatives in England. It was this conception of individual liberty under the law which in the first instance inspired the liberal movements on the Continent and which became the basis of the American political tradition. A few of the leading political thinkers in those countries like B. Constant and A. de Tocqueville in France, Immanuel Kant, Friedrich von Schiller and Wilhelm von Humboldt in Germany, and James Madison, John Marshall and Daniel Webster in the United States belong wholly to it.

This liberalism must be clearly distinguished from another, originally Continental European tradition, also called 'liberalism' of which what now claims this name in the United States is a direct descendant. This latter view, though beginning with an attempt to imitate the first tradition, interpreted it in the spirit of a constructivist rationalism prevalent in France and thereby made of it something very different, and in the end, instead of advocating limitations on the powers of government, ended up with the ideal of the unlimited powers of the majority. This is the tradition of Voltaire, Rousseau, Condorcet and the French Revolution which became the ancestor of modern socialism. English utilitarianism has taken over much of this Continental tradition and the late-nineteenth-century British liberal party, resulting from a fusion of the liberal Whigs and the utilitarian Radicals, was also a product of this mixture.

Liberalism and democracy, although compatible, are not the

same. The first is concerned with the extent of governmental power, the second with who holds this power. The difference is best seen if we consider their opposites: the opposite of liberalism is totalitarianism, while the opposite of democracy is authoritarianism. In consequence, it is at least possible in principle that a democratic government may be totalitarian and that an authoritarian government may act on liberal principles. The second kind of 'liberalism' mentioned before has in effect become democratism rather than liberalism and, demanding *unlimited* power of the majority, has become essentially anti-liberal.

It should be specially emphasized that the two political philosophies which both describe themselves as 'liberalism' and lead in a few respects to similar conclusions, rest on altogether different philosophical foundations. The first is based on an evolutionary interpretation of all phenomena of culture and mind and on an insight into the limits of the powers of the human reason. The second rests on what I have called 'constructivist' rationalism, a conception which leads to the treatment of all cultural phenomena as the product of deliberate design, and on the belief that it is both possible and desirable to reconstruct all grown institutions in accordance with a preconceived plan. The first kind is consequently reverent of tradition and recognizes that all knowledge and all civilization rests on tradition, while the second type is contemptuous of tradition because it regards an independently existing reason as capable of designing civilization. (Cf. the statement by Voltaire: 'If you want good laws, burn those you have and make new ones.') The first is also an essentially modest creed, relying on abstraction as the only available means to extend the limited powers of reason, while the second refuses to recognize any such limits and believes that reason alone can prove the desirability of particular concrete arrangements.

(It is a result of this difference that the first kind of liberalism is at least not incompatible with religious beliefs and has often been held and even been developed by men holding strong religious beliefs, while the 'Continental' type of liberalism has always been antagonistic to all religion and politically in constant conflict with organized religions.)

The first kind of liberalism, which we shall henceforth alone consider, is itself not the result of a theoretical construction but arose from the desire to extend and generalize the beneficial effects which unexpectedly had followed on the limitations placed on the powers of government out of sheer distrust of the rulers. Only after it was found that the unquestioned greater personal liberty which the Englishman enjoyed in the eighteenth century had produced an unprecedented material prosperity were attempts made to develop a systematic theory of liberalism, attempts which in England never were carried very far, while the Continental interpretations largely changed the meaning of the English tradition.

Liberalism thus derives from the discovery of a self-generating or spontaneous order in social affairs (the same discovery which led to the recognition that there existed an object for theoretical social sciences), an order which made it possible to utilize the knowledge and skill of all members of society to a much greater extent than would be possible in any order created by central direction, and the consequent desire to make as full use of these powerful spontaneous ordering forces as possible.

It was thus in their efforts to make explicit the principles of an order already existing but only in an imperfect form that Adam Smith and his followers developed the basic principles of liberalism in order to demonstrate the desirability of their general application. In doing this they were able to presuppose familiarity with the common law conception of justice and with the ideals of the rule of law and of government under the law which were little understood outside the Anglo-Saxon world; with the result that not only were their ideas not fully understood outside the English-speaking countries, but that they ceased to be fully understood even in England when Bentham and his followers replaced the English legal tradition by a constructivist utilitarianism derived more from Continental rationalism than from the evolutionary conception of the English tradition.

The central concept of liberalism is that under the enforcement of universal rules of just conduct, protecting a recognizable private domain of individuals, a spontaneous order of human activities of much greater complexity will form itself than could ever be produced by deliberate arrangement, and that in consequence the coercive activities of government should be limited to the enforcement of such rules, whatever other services government may at the same time render by administering those particular resources which have been placed at its disposal for those purposes.

The distinction between a *spontaneous order* based on abstract rules which leave individuals free to use their own knowledge for their own purposes, and an *organization or arrangement* based on commands, is of central importance for the understanding of the principles of a free society and must in the following paragraphs be explained in some detail, especially as the spontaneous order of a free society will contain many organizations (including the biggest organization, government), but the two principles of order cannot be mixed in any manner we may wish.

The first peculiarity of a spontaneous order is that by using its ordering forces (the regularity of the conduct of its members) we can achieve an order of a much more complex set of facts than we could ever achieve by deliberate arrangement, but that, while availing ourselves of this possibility of inducing an order of much greater extent than we otherwise could, we at the same time limit our power over the details of that order. We shall say that when using the former principle we shall have power only over the abstract character but not over the concrete detail of that order.

No less important is the fact that, in contrast to an organization, neither has a spontaneous order a purpose nor need there be agreement on the concrete results it will produce in order to agree on the desirability of such an order, because, being independent of any particular purpose, it can be used for, and will assist in the pursuit of, a great many different, divergent and even conflicting individual purposes. Thus the order of the market, in particular, rests not on common purposes but on reciprocity, that is on the reconciliation of different purposes for the mutual benefit of the participants.

The conception of the common welfare or of the public good of a free society can therefore never be defined as a sum of known particular results to be achieved, but only as an abstract order which as a whole is not oriented on any particular concrete ends but provides merely the best chance for any member selected at random successfully to use his knowledge for his purposes. Adopting a term of Professor Michael Oakeshott (London), we may call such a free society a *nomocratic* (law-governed) as distinguished from an unfree *telocratic* (purpose-governed) social order.

The great importance of the spontaneous order or nomocracy rests on the fact that it extends the possibility of peaceful co-existence of men for their mutual benefit beyond the small group whose members have concrete common purposes, or were subject to a common superior, and that it thus made the appearance of the *Great* or *Open Society* possible. This order which has progressively grown beyond the organizations of the family, the horde, the clan and the tribe, the principalities and even the empire or national state, and has produced at least the beginning of a world society, is based on the adoption – without and often against the desire of political authority – of rules which came to prevail because the groups who observed them were more successful; and it has existed and grown in extent long before men were aware of its existence or understood its operation.

The spontaneous order of the market, based on reciprocity or mutual benefits, is commonly described as an economic order; and in the vulgar sense of the term 'economic' the Great Society is indeed held together entirely by what are commonly called economic forces. But it is exceedingly misleading, and has become one of the chief sources of confusion and misunderstanding, to call this order an economy as we do when we speak of a national, social, or world economy. This is at least one of the chief sources of most socialist endeavour to turn the spontaneous order of the market into a deliberately run organization serving an agreed system of common ends.

An economy in the strict sense of the word in which we can call a household, a farm, an enterprise or even the financial administration of government an economy, is indeed an organization or a deliberate arrangement of a given stock of resources in the service of a unitary order of purposes. It rests on a system of coherent decisions in which a single view of the relative importance of the different competing purposes determines the uses to be made of the different resources.

The spontaneous order of the market resulting from the inter-action of many such economies is something so fundamentally different from an economy proper that it must be regarded as a great misfortune that it has ever been called by the same name. I have become convinced that this practice so constantly mis-leads people that it is necessary to invent a new technical term for it. I propose that we call this spontaneous order of the market a *catallaxy* in analogy to the term 'catallactics', which has often been proposed as a substitute for the term 'economics'. (Both 'catallaxy' and 'catallactics' derive from the ancient Greek verb *katallattein* which, significantly, means not only 'to barter' and 'to exchange' but also 'to admit into the communi-ty' and 'to turn from enemy into friend'.)

The chief point about the catallaxy is that, as a spontaneous order, its orderliness does *not* rest on its orientation on a single hierarchy of ends, and that, therefore, it will *not* secure that for it as a whole the more important comes before the less impor-tant. This is the chief cause of its condemnation by its oppo-nents, and it could be said that most of the socialist demands amount to nothing less than that the catallaxy should be turned into an economy proper (i.e. the purposeless spontaneous order into a purpose-oriented organization) in order to assure that the more important be never sacrificed to the less important. The defence of the free society must therefore show that it is due to the fact that we do not enforce a unitary scale of concrete ends, nor attempt to secure that some particular view about what is more and what is less important governs the whole of society, that the members of such a free society have as good a chance successfully to use their individual knowledge for the achieve-ment of their individual purposes as they in fact have.

The extension of an order of peace beyond the small purpose-oriented organization became thus possible by the extension of purpose-independent ('formal') rules of just conduct to the re-lations with other men who did not pursue the same concrete ends or hold the same values except those abstract rules – rules which did not impose obligations for particular actions (which always presuppose a concrete end) but consisted solely in prohi-bitions from infringing the protected domain of each which these rules enable us to determine. Liberalism is therefore inseparable from the institution of private property which is the name we usually give to the material part of this protected individual domain.

But if liberalism presupposes the enforcement of rules of just conduct and expects a desirable spontaneous order to form itself only if appropriate rules of just conduct are in fact observed, it also wants to restrict the *coercive* powers of government to the enforcement of such rules of just conduct, including at least one prescribing a positive duty, namely, the rule requiring citizens to contribute according to uniform principles not only to the cost of enforcing those rules but also to the costs of the non-coercive service functions of government which we shall presently consider. Liberalism is therefore the same as the demand for the rule of law in the classical sense of the term according to which the coercive functions of government are strictly limited to the enforcement of uniform rules of law, meaning uniform rules of just conduct towards one's fellows. (The "rule of law" corresponds here to what in German is called *materieller Rechtsstaat* as distinguished from the mere *formelle Rechtsstaat* which requires only that each act of government is authorized by legislation, whether such a law consists of a general rule of just conduct or not.)

Liberalism recognizes that there are certain other services which for various reasons the spontaneous forces of the market may not produce or may not produce adequately, and that for this reason it is desirable to put at the disposal of government a clearly circumscribed body of resources with which it can render such services to the citizens in general. This requires a sharp distinction between the coercive powers of government, in which its actions are strictly limited to the enforcement of rules of just conduct and in the exercise of which all discretion is excluded, and the provision of services by government, for which it can use only the resources put at its disposal for this purpose, has no coercive power or monopoly, but in the use of which resources it enjoys wide discretion.

It is significant that such a conception of a liberal order has arisen only in countries in which, in ancient Greece and Rome no less than in modern Britain, justice was conceived as something to be discovered by the efforts of judges or scholars and not as determined by the arbitrary will of any authority; that it always had difficulty in taking roots in countries in which law was conceived primarily as the product of deliberate legislation, and that it has everywhere declined under the joint influence of legal positivism and of democratic doctrine, both of which know no other criterion of justice than the will of the legislator.

Liberalism has indeed inherited from the theories of the common law and from the older (pre-rationalist) theories of the law of nature, and also presupposes a conception of justice which allows us to distinguish between such rules of just individual conduct as are implied in the conception of the 'rule of law' and are required for the formation of a spontaneous order on the one hand, and all the particular commands issued by authority for the purpose of organization on the other. This essential distinction has been made explicit in the legal theories of two of the greatest philosophers of modern times, David Hume and Immanuel Kant, but has not been adequately restated since and is wholly uncongenial to the governing legal theories of our day.

The essential points of this conception of justice are (a) that justice can be meaningfully attributed only to human action and not to any state of affairs as such without reference to the question whether it has been, or could have been, deliberately brought about by somebody; (b) that the rules of justice have essentially the nature of prohibitions, or, in other words, that injustice is really the primary concept and the aim of rules of just conduct is to prevent unjust action; (c) that the injustice to be prevented is the infringement of the protected domain of one's fellow men, a domain which is to be ascertained by means of these rules of justice; and (d) that these rules of just conduct which are in themselves negative can be developed by consistently applying to whatever such rules a society has inherited the equally negative test of universal applicability – a test which, in the last resort, is nothing other than the self-consistency of the actions which these rules allow if applied to the circumstances of the real world. These four crucial points must be developed further in the following paragraphs.

Ad (*a*): Rules of just conduct can require the individual to take into account in his decisions only such consequences of his actions as he himself can foresee. The concrete results of the catallaxy for particular people are, however, essentially unpredictable; and since they are not the effect of anyone's design or intentions, it is meaningless to describe the manner in which the market distributed the good things of this world among particular people as just or unjust. This, however, is what the so-called 'social' or 'distributive' justice aims at and in the name of which the liberal order of law is progressively destroyed. We shall later see that no test or criteria have been found or can be found by which such rules of 'social justice' can be assessed, and that, in consequence, and in contrast to the rules of just conduct, they would have to be determined by the arbitrary will of the holders of power.

Ad (*b*): No particular human action is fully determined without a concrete purpose it is meant to achieve. Free men who are to be allowed to use their own means and their own knowledge for their own purposes must therefore not be subject to rules which tell them what they must positively do, but only to rules which tell them what they must not do; except for the discharge of obligations an individual has voluntarily incurred, the rules of just conduct thus merely delimit the range of permissible actions but do not determine the particular actions a man must take at a particular moment. (There are certain rare exceptions to this, like actions to save or protect life, prevent catastrophes, and the like, where either rules of justice actually do require, or would at least generally be accepted as just rules if they did require, some positive action. It would lead far to discuss here the position of such rules in the system.) The generally negative character of the rules of just conduct, and the corresponding primacy of the injustice which is prohibited, has often been noticed but scarcely ever been thought through to its logical consequences.

Ad (*c*): The injustice which is prohibited by rules of just conduct is any encroachment on the protected domain of other individuals, and they must therefore enable us to ascertain what is the protected sphere of others. Since the time of John Locke it is customary to describe this protected domain as property (which Locke himself had defined as 'the life, liberty, and possessions of a man'). This term suggests, however, a much too narrow and purely material conception of the protected domain which includes not only material goods but also various claims on others and certain expectations. If the concept of property is, however, (with Locke) interpreted in this wide sense, it is true that law, in the sense of rules of justice, and the institution of property are inseparable.

Ad (d): It is impossible to decide about the justice of any one particular rule of just conduct except within the framework of a whole system of such rules, most of which must for this purpose be regarded as unquestioned: values can always be tested only in terms of other values. The test of the justice of a rule is usually (since Kant) described as that of its 'universalizability', i.e., of the possibility of willing that the rules should be applied to all instances that correspond to the conditions stated in it (the 'categorical imperative'). What this amounts to is that in applying it to any concrete circumstances it will not conflict with any other accepted rules. The test is thus in the last resort one of the compatibility or non-contradictoriness of the whole system of rules, not merely in a logical sense but in the sense that the system of actions which the rules permit will not lead to conflict.

It will be noticed that only purpose-independent ('formal') rules pass this test because, as rules which have originally been developed in small, purpose-connected groups ('organizations') are progressively extended to larger and larger groups and finally universalized to apply to the relations between any members of an Open Society who have no concrete purposes in common and merely submit to the same abstract rules, they will in this process have to shed all references to particular purposes.

The growth from the tribal organization, all of whose members served common purposes, to the spontaneous order of the Open Society in which people are allowed to pursue their own purposes in peace, may thus be said to have commenced when for the first time a savage placed some goods at the boundary of his tribe in the hope that some member of another tribe would find them and leave in turn behind some other goods to secure the repetition of the offer. From the first establishment of such a practice which served reciprocal but not common purposes, a process has been going on for millennia which, by making rules of conduct independent of the particular purposes of those concerned, made it possible to extend these rules to ever wider circles of undetermined persons and eventually might make possible a universal peaceful order of the world.

The character of those universal rules of just individual conduct, which liberalism presupposes and wishes to improve as much as possible, has been obscured by confusion with that other part of law which determines the organization of government and guides it in the administration of the resources placed at its disposal. It is a characteristic of liberal society that the private individual can be coerced to obey only the rules of private and criminal law; and the progressive permeation of private law by public law in the course of the last eighty or hundred years, which means a progressive replacement of rules of conduct by rules of organization, is one of the main ways in which the destruction of the liberal order has been effected. A German scholar (Franz Böhm) has for this reason recently described the liberal order very justly as the *Privatrechtsgesellschaft* (private law society).

The difference between the order at which the rules of conduct of private and criminal law aim, and the order at which the rules of organization of public law aim, comes out most clearly if we consider that rules of conduct will determine an order of action only in combination with the particular knowledge and aims of the acting individuals, while the rules of organization of public law determine directly such concrete action in the light of particular purposes, or, rather, give some authority power to do so. The confusion between rules of conduct and rules of organization has been assisted by an erroneous identification of what is often called the 'order of law' with the order of actions, which in a free system is not fully determined by the system of laws but merely presupposes such system of laws as one of the conditions required for its formation. Not every system of rules of conduct which secures uniformity of action (which is how the 'order of law' is frequently interpreted) will, however, secure an order of action in the sense that the actions permitted by the rules will not conflict.

The progressive displacement of the rules of conduct of private and criminal law by a conception derived from public law is the process by which existing liberal societies are progressively transformed into totalitarian societies. This tendency has been most explicitly seen and supported by Adolf Hitler's 'crown jurist' Carl Schmitt who consistently advocated the replacement of the 'normative' thinking of liberal law by a conception of law which regards as its purpose the 'concrete order formation' (*konkretes Ordnungsdenken*).

Historically this development has become possible as a result of the fact that the same representative assemblies have been charged with the two different tasks of laying down rules of individual conduct and laying down rules and giving orders concerning the organization and conduct of government. The consequence of this has been that the term 'law' itself, which in the older conception of the 'rule of law' had meant only rules of conduct equally applicable to all, came to mean any rule of organization or even any particular command approved by the constitutionally appointed legislature. Such a conception of the rule of law which merely demands that a command be legitimately issued and not that it be a rule of justice equally applicable to all (what the Germans call the merely *formelle Rechsstaat*), of course no longer provides any protection of individual freedom.

If it was the nature of the constitutional arrangements prevailing in all Western democracies which made this development possible, the driving force which guided it in the particular direction was the growing recognition that the application of uniform or equal rules to the conduct of individuals who were in fact very different in many respects, inevitably produced very different results for the different individuals; and that in order to bring about by government action a reduction in these unintended but inevitable differences in the material position of different people, it would be necessary to treat them not according to the same but according to different rules. This gave rise to a new and altogether different conception of justice, namely that usually described as 'social' or 'distributive' justice, a conception of justice which did not confine itself to rules of conduct for the individual but aimed at particular results for particular people, and which therefore could be achieved only in a purpose-governed organization but not in a purpose-independent spontaneous order.

The concepts of a 'just price', a 'just remuneration' or a

'just distribution of incomes' are of course very old; it deserves notice, however, that in the course of the efforts of two thousand years in which philosophers have speculated about the meaning of these concepts, not a single rule has been discovered which would allow us to determine what is in this sense just in a market order. Indeed the one group of scholars which have most persistently pursued the question, the schoolmen of the later middle ages and early modern times, were finally driven to define the just price or wage as that price or wage which would form itself on a market in the absence of fraud, violence or privilege – thus referring back to the rules of just conduct and accepting as a just result whatever was brought about by the just conduct of all individuals concerned. This negative conclusion of all the speculations about 'social' or 'distributive' justice was, as we shall see, inevitable, because a just remuneration or distribution has meaning only within an organization whose members act under command in the service of a common system of ends, but can have no meaning whatever in a catallaxy or spontaneous order which can have no such common system of ends.

A state of affairs as such, as we have seen, cannot be just or unjust as a mere fact. Only in so far as it has been brought about designedly or could be so brought about does it make sense to call just or unjust the actions of those who have created it or permitted it to arise. In the catallaxy, the spontaneous order of the market, nobody can foresee, however, what each participant will get, and the results for particular people are not determined by anyone's intentions; nor is anyone responsible for particular people getting particular things. We might therefore question whether a deliberate choice of the market order as the method for guiding economic activities, with the unpredictable and, in a great measure, chance incidence of its benefits, is a just decision, but certainly not whether, once we have decided to avail ourselves of the catallaxy for that purpose, the particular results it produces for particular people are just or unjust.

That the concept of justice is nevertheless so commonly and readily applied to the distribution of incomes is entirely the effect of an erroneous anthropomorphic interpretation of society as an organization rather than as a spontaneous order. The term 'distribution' is in this sense quite as misleading as the term 'economy', since it also suggests that something is the result of deliberate action which in fact is the result of spontaneous ordering forces. Nobody distributes income in a market order (as would have to be done in an organization) and to speak, with respect to the former, of a just or unjust distribution is therefore simple nonsense. It would be less misleading to speak in this respect of a 'dispersion' rather than a 'distribution' of incomes.

All endeavours to secure a 'just' distribution must thus be directed towards turning the spontaneous order of the market into an organization or, in other words, into a totalitarian order. It was this striving after a new conception of justice which produced the various steps by which rules of organization ('public law'), which were designed to make people aim at particular results, came to supersede the purpose-independent rules of just individual conduct, and which thereby gradually destroyed the foundations on which a spontaneous order must rest.

The ideal of using the coercive powers of government to achieve 'positive' (i.e., social or distributive) justice leads, however, not only necessarily to the destruction of individual freedom, which some might not think too high a price, but it also proves on examination a mirage or an illusion which cannot be achieved in any circumstances, because it presupposes an agreement on the relative importance of the different concrete ends which cannot exist in a great society whose members do not know each other or the same particular facts. It is sometimes believed that the fact that most people today desire social justice demonstrates that this ideal has a determinable content. But it is unfortunately only too possible to chase a mirage, and the consequence of this is always that the result of one's striving will be utterly different from what one had intended.

There can be no rules which determine how much everybody 'ought' to have unless we make some unitary conception of relative 'merits' or 'needs' of the different individuals, for which there exists no objective measure, the basis of a central allocation of all goods and services – which would make it necessary that each individual, instead of using *his* knowledge for *his* purposes, be made to fulfil a duty imposed upon him by somebody else, and be remunerated according to how well he has, in the opinion of others, performed this duty. This is the method of remuneration appropriate to a closed organization, such as an army, but irreconcilable with the forces which maintain a spontaneous order.

It ought to be freely admitted that the market order does not bring about any close correspondence between subjective merit or individual needs and rewards. It operates on the principle of a combined game of skill and chance in which the results for each individual may be as much determined by circumstances wholly beyond his control as by his skill or effort. Each is remunerated according to the value his particular services have to the particular people to whom he renders them, and this value of his services stands in no necessary relation to anything which we could appropriately call his merits and still less to his needs.

It deserves special emphasis that, strictly speaking, it is meaningless to speak of a value 'to society' when what is in question is the value of some services to certain people, services which may be of no interest to anybody else. A violin virtuoso presumably renders services to entirely different people from those whom a football star entertains, and the maker of pipes to altogether different people from the maker of perfumes. The whole conception of a 'value to society' is in a free order as illegitimate an anthropomorphic term as its description as 'one economy' in the strict sense or as an entity which 'treats' people justly or unjustly, or 'distributes' among them. The results of the market process for particular individuals are neither the result of anybody's will that they should have so much, nor even foreseeable by those who have decided upon or support the maintenance of this kind of order.

Of all the complaints about the injustice of the results of the market order the one which appears to have had the greatest effect on actual policy, and to have produced a progressive destruction of the equal rules of just conduct and their replacement by a 'social' law aiming at 'social justice', however, was not the extent of the inequality of the rewards, nor their disproportion with recognizable merits, needs, efforts, pains incurred, or whatever else has been chiefly stressed by social philosophers, but the demands for protection against an undeserved descent from an already achieved position. More than by anything else the market order has been distorted by efforts to protect groups from a decline from their former position; and when government interference is demanded in the name of 'social justice' this now means, more often than not, the demand for the protection of the existing relative position of some group. 'Social justice' has thus become little more than a demand for the protection of vested interests and the creation of new privilege, such as when in the name of social justice the farmer is assured 'parity' with the industrial worker.

The important facts to be stressed here are that the positions thus protected were the result of the same sort of forces as those which now reduce the relative position of the same people, that their position for which they now demand protection was no more deserved or earned than the diminished position now in prospect for them, and that their former position could in the changed position be secured to them only by denying to others the same chances of ascent to which they owed their former position. In a market order the fact that a group of persons has achieved a certain relative position cannot give them a claim in justice to maintain it, because this cannot be defended by a rule which could be equally applied to all.

The aim of economic policy of a free society can therefore never be to assure particular results to particular people, and its success cannot be measured by any attempt at adding up the value of such particular results. In this respect the aim of what is called 'welfare economics' is fundamentally mistaken, not only because no meaningful sum can be formed of the satisfactions provided for different people, but because its basic idea of a maximum of need-fulfilment (or a maximum social product) is appropriate only to an economy proper which serves a single hierarchy of ends, but not to the spontaneous order of a catallaxy which has no common concrete ends.

Though it is widely believed that the conception of an optimal economic policy (or any judgment whether one economic policy is better than another) presupposes such a conception of maximizing aggregate real social income (which is possible only in value terms and therefore implies an illegitimate comparison of the utility to different persons), this is in fact not so. An optimal policy in a catallaxy may aim, and ought to aim, at increasing the chances of any member of society taken at random of having a high income, or, what amounts to the same thing, the chance that, whatever his share in total income may be, the real equivalent of this share will be as large as we know how to make it.

This condition will be approached as closely as we can manage, irrespective of the dispersion of incomes, if everything which is produced is being produced by persons or organizations who can produce it more cheaply than (or at least as cheaply as) anybody who does not produce it, and is sold at a price lower than that at which it would be possible to offer it for anybody who does not in fact so offer it. (This allows for persons or organizations to whom the costs of producing one commodity or service are lower than they are for those who actually produce it and who still produce something else instead, because their comparative advantage in that other production is still greater; in this case the total costs of their producing the first commodity would have to include the loss of the one which is not produced.)

It will be noticed that this optimum does not presuppose what economic theory calls 'perfect competition' but only that there are no obstacles to the entry into each trade and that the market functions adequately in spreading information about opportunities. It should also be specially observed that this modest and achievable goal has never yet been fully achieved because at all times and everywhere governments have both restricted access to some occupations and tolerated persons and organizations deterring others from entering occupations when this would have been to the advantage of the latter.

This optimum position means that as much will be produced, of whatever combination of products and services is in fact produced, as can be produced by any method that we know, because we can through such a use of the market mechanism bring more of the dispersed knowledge of the members of society into play than by any other. But it will be achieved only if we leave the share in the total, which each member will get, to be determined by the market mechanism and all its accidents, because it is

only through the market determination of incomes that each is
led to do what this result requires.

We owe, in other words, our chances that our unpredictable
share in the total product of society represents as large an aggregate of goods and services as it does to the fact that thousands of
others constantly submit to the adjustments which the market
forces on them; and it is consequently also our duty to accept
the same kind of changes in our income and position, even if it
means a decline in our accustomed position and is due to circumstances we could not have foreseen and for which we are not
responsible. The conception that we have 'earned' (in the sense
of morally deserved) the income we had when we were more
fortunate, and that we are therefore entitled to it so long as we
strive as honestly as before and had no warning to turn elsewhere, is wholly mistaken. Everybody, rich or poor, owes his
income to the outcome of a mixed game of skill and chance, the
aggregate result of which and the shares in which are as high as
they are only because we have agreed to play that game. And
once we have agreed to play the game and profited from its results, it is a moral obligation on us to abide by the results even if
they turn against us.

There can be little doubt that in modern society all but the
most unfortunate and those who in a different kind of society
might have enjoyed a legal privilege, owe to the adoption of
that method an income much larger than they could otherwise
enjoy. There is of course no reason why a society which, thanks
to the market, is as rich as modern society should not provide
outside the market a minimum security for all who in the market
fall below a certain standard. Our point was merely that considerations of justice provide no justification for 'correcting'
the results of the market and that justice, in the sense of treatment under the same rules, requires that each takes what a
market provides in which every participant behaves fairly.
There is only a justice of individual conduct but not a separate
'social justice'.

We cannot consider here the legitimate tasks of government
in the administration of the resources placed at its disposal for
the rendering of services to the citizens. With regard to these
functions, for the discharge of which the government is given

money, we will here only say that in exercising them government should be under the same rules as every private citizen, that it should possess no monopoly for a particular service of this kind, that it should discharge these functions in such a manner as not to disturb the much more comprehensive spontaneously ordered efforts of society, and that the means should be raised according to a rule which applies uniformly to all. (This, in my opinion, precludes an overall progression of the burden of taxation of the individual, since such a use of taxation for purposes of redistribution could be justified only by such arguments as we have just excluded.) In the remaining paragraphs we shall be concerned only with some of the functions of government for the discharge of which it is given not merely money but power to enforce rules of private conduct.

The only part of these coercive functions of government which we can further consider in this outline are those which are concerned with the preservation of a functioning market order. They concern primarily the conditions which must be provided by law to secure the degree of competition required to steer the market efficiently. We shall briefly consider this question first with regard to enterprise and then with regard to labour.

With regard to enterprise the first point which needs underlining is that it is more important that government refrain from assisting monopolies than that it combat monopoly. If today the market order is confined only to a part of the economic activities of men, this is largely the result of deliberate government restrictions of competition. It is indeed doubtful whether, if government consistently refrained from creating monopolies and from assisting them through protective tariffs and the character of the law of patents for inventions and of the law of corporations, there would remain an element of monopoly significant enough to require special measures. What must be chiefly remembered in this connection is, firstly, that monopolistic positions are always undesirable but often unavoidable for objective reasons which we cannot or do not wish to alter; and, secondly, that all government-supervised monopolies tend to become government-protected monopolies which will persist when their justification has disappeared.

Current conceptions of anti-monopoly policy are largely misguided by the application of certain conceptions developed by the theory of perfect competition which are irrelevant to conditions where the factual presuppositions of the theory of perfect competition are absent. The theory of perfect competition shows that if on a market the number of buyers and sellers is sufficiently large to make it impossible for any one of them deliberately to influence prices, such quantities will be sold at prices which will equal marginal costs. This does not mean, however, that it is either possible or even necessarily desirable everywhere to bring about a state of affairs where large numbers buy and sell the same uniform commodity. The idea that in situations where we cannot, or do not wish to, bring about such a state, the producers should be held to conduct themselves as if perfect competition existed, or to sell at a price which would rule under perfect competition, is meaningless, because we do not know what would be the particular conduct required, or the price which would be formed, if perfect competition existed.

Where the conditions for perfect competition do not exist, what competition still can and ought to be made to achieve is nevertheless very remarkable and important, namely the conditions described in the above paragraphs. It was pointed out then that this state will tend to be approached if nobody can be prevented by government or others from entering any trade or occupation he desires.

This condition would, I believe, be approached as closely as it is possible to do so if, *firstly*, all agreements to restrain trade were without exception (not prohibited, but merely) made void and unenforceable, and, *secondly*, all discriminatory or other actions aimed towards an actual or potential competitor and intended to make him observe certain rules of market conduct were to be made liable for multiple damages. It seems to me that such a modest aim would produce a much more effective law than actual prohibitions under penalties, because no exceptions need to be made from such a declaration as invalid or unenforceable of all contracts in restraint of trade, while, as experience has shown, the more ambitious attempts are bound to be qualified by so many exceptions as to make them much less effective.

The application of this same principle that all agreements in restraint of trade should be invalid and unenforceable and that every individual should be protected against all attempts to enforce them by violence or aimed discrimination, is even more important with regard to labour. The monopolistic practices which threaten the functioning of the market are today much more serious on the side of labour than on the side of enterprise, and the preservation of the market order will depend, more than on anything else, on whether we succeed in curbing the latter.

The reason for this is that the developments in this field are bound to force government, and are already forcing many governments, into two kinds of measures which are wholly destructive of the market order: attempts authoritatively to determine the appropriate incomes of the various groups (by what is called an 'incomes policy') and efforts to overcome the wage 'rigidities' by an inflationary monetary policy. But since this evasion of the real issue by only temporarily effective monetary means must have the effect that those 'rigidities' will constantly increase, they are a mere palliative which can only postpone but not solve the central problem.

Monetary and financial policy is outside the scope of this paper. Its problems were mentioned only to point out that its fundamental and, in the present situation, insoluble dilemmas cannot be solved by any monetary means but only by a restoration of the market as an effective instrument for determining wages.

In conclusion, the basic principles of a liberal society may be summed up by saying that in such a society all coercive functions of government must be guided by the overruling importance of what I like to call *The Three Great Negatives; Peace, Justice and Liberty*. Their achievement requires that in its coercive functions government shall be confined to the enforcement of such prohibitions (stated as abstract rules) as can be equally applied to all, and to exacting under the same uniform rules from all a share of the costs of the other, noncoercive services it may decide to render to the citizens with the material and personal means thereby placed as its disposal.

Socialism

GEORGE DOUGLAS HOWARD COLE

G. D. H. Cole was born in Cambridge in 1889 and educated at Balliol College, Oxford. An advocate of guild socialism he was chairman of the Fabian Society for many years. In 1952 he became president of the society, a position he occupied until his death in 1959. He held academic posts at the University of London and the University of Oxford. In 1944 he was appointed Chichele Professor of Social and Political Theory.

His publications include: *Self-Government in Industry*, 1917; *Guild Socialism Re-Stated*, 1920; *A Century of Co-operation*, 1946; *The Intelligent Man's Guide to the Post-War World*, 1947; *Local and Regional Government*, 1942; *A History of Socialist Thought*, 7 vols. 1st vol. 1953; *Post-War Condition of Britain*, 1956.

What is Socialism?

G. D. H. Cole

What is socialism? There have been so many notions of it; but if the name has any real meaning there must be some common element, however elusive it may be. The word has been in frequent use for upwards of a century in both French and English: in which of the two countries it originated is still uncertain. It seems to have been used first – apart from a single earlier use in Italian in an entirely different sense – at some time in the second half of the 1820s, and to have passed quickly into fairly general use to describe certain theories or systems of social organization. 'Socialists' were the persons who advocated these theories or systems. Alternatively such persons were called 'Owenites', or 'Fourierists', or 'Saint-Simonians', or by a variety of other names derived either from the originators of particular systems or from the names these originators gave to them – for example, 'Harmonists', or 'Associationists', or 'Icarians' – this last after Cabet's projected Utopia, described in his *Voyage en Icarie* (1840). Jérome Blanqui, the economist, brother of the better-known revolutionary, Auguste Blanqui, dubbed them all 'Utopians': Karl Marx took up the word, and grouped them in the *Communist Manifesto* of 1848 as 'Utopian Socialists', by way of distinguishing their doctrines from his own 'Scientific Socialism'. Thereafter there were said to be two sorts of 'Socialism' – 'Utopian' and 'Scientific'. To these was soon to be added a third kind, Libertarian or Anarchist, of which in their several ways Proudhon and Bakunin were the pioneers. Later still came a fourth kind, often called Fabian or Evolutionary Socialism, differentiated from Marx's Scientific Socialism by its belief in what is termed 'gradualism' – the creed of most of the western Labour and Socialist parties of today. What had all these kinds of socialism in common, to be called by the same name? The answer, in brief, is – hostility to *laissez-faire* and economic competition, and belief in some sort of collective or co-operative action as a means of improving the condition of the many poor.

The 'Utopian' Socialists whom Marx claimed to supersede were all essentially moralists. They set out, some with more and some with less regard for time and place, to prescribe the conditions needed for the establishment of the 'good society', or of 'good societies' which would enable men to escape the evils of the actual societies in which they were living. It was a common view of all of them that existing societies were corrupt and corrupting to their citizens, and that the possibility of living a good life depended on devising and establishing a right structure of human relations. Most, if not all, of them believed that in some valid sense good living was 'natural', and bad living a consequence of artificial departure from 'natural' conditions. Most, if not all, of them, while they roundly denounced the abuses of existing societies, at the same time believed in progress as 'natural', and were optimists about the future of humanity. Most, if not all, of them also believed that a great advance in the art of living was on the point of being achieved, and connected the prospect of this advance with the progress made in human knowledge. Some of them stressed the intellectual aspect of this progress; others the technological. Most of them believed that the development of science and of the techniques of production had put mankind into a position to solve once and for all the problem of poverty, by producing enough to provide the means of natural good living for the entire human race. Most of them held in addition that men tended to become more rational in action as their knowledge increased, and that the application of reason to politics was destined speedily to revolutionize human relations. Many of them identified knowledge with virtue, or at any rate held that to know the good was virtually the same thing as to act rightly. In this spirit they projected their Utopias, in the confidence that rightly adjusted social structures could not fail to induce men to behave reasonably and to co-operate in making these structures work well.

Thus the 'socialists' of the early part of the nineteenth century were moral reformers who held that the clue to moral reformation was to be sought in the reformation of the social order. They were 'socialists', first and foremost, because they put the main stress on social arrangements as the operative causes of good and bad living, and of individual virtue or vice. They tended to regard evil conduct as a consequence less of individual sins or shortcomings than of a bad, 'unnatural' environment. Get the environment right, they said, and most men will behave decently and reasonably in their mutual affairs. They differed, indeed, to some extent concerning the process by which the change in individual behaviour would come about. Some, such as Owen and Saint-Simon, emphasized the influence of education on the formation of character, and assigned great importance to rational education as a factor in the making of the new society. Others, especially Fourier, argued that there was no need for any change in human nature, because all men's passions, including those which in existing societies led to anti-social conduct, would work for good in a society organized to fit in with men's natural propensities. But this difference, important though it was, did not prevent them from agreeing that the essential thing was not to preach virtue to individuals so much as to establish an environment in which there would be the greatest possible encouragement to men to act virtuously, because the system of expectations surrounding the individual would be such as to make virtue come easy to him, and vice difficult.

'Utopian Socialism', then made its début as a plan for a system of social organization designed to further human happiness and well-being by the facilitating of good behaviour. All its proponents agreed that existing societies, far from doing this, gave most men strong temptations to act anti-socially. They differed in the stresses they put on different aspects of the evils of society as it was; some of them denounced 'privilege' as the principal cause of social ills, others 'competition'. The former pointed out how the system of privilege for a limited group within society was inconsistent with the fundamentally equal right of all men to pursue happiness and well-being, because it involved a structure of preferential 'rights' and therewith a denial of the rights of the many in deference to the claims of the few. Some – for example Saint-Simon – also argued that it was manifestly wrong for privilege, if it were to be accorded at all, to go to the unproductive (*les oisifs*) at the expense of the productive (*les industriels*). Others, such as Owen and the 'left-Ricardian' economists who preceded Marx, stressed chiefly the evils of competition, as encouraging men to contend against men, instead of fostering habits of mutual co-operation in a common pursuit of the good life. Which of these arguments got most emphasis depended largely on the kind of society the reformers were thinking of as needing to be overthrown. Against the *ancien régime* it was natural to stress the iniquities of privilege: against the rising capitalist system the evils of competition in money-making. Wherever the stress was put, the 'socialists' were at one in denouncing the exploitation of the real producers of wealth by the ruling classes, and in demanding that in the new society co-operation, and not mutual antagonism and conflict, should be the guiding principle of social organization.

It has sometimes been said that the 'Utopian' Socialists differed from their successors in having no notion of socialism as a 'class-issue'. This is true only in a qualified sense. Many of them were acutely conscious of the exploitation of the working classes under the existing social order and of the unjustifiable privileges of the superior classes. Indeed, I think they all denounced this exploitation, though they did not all think of it in the same terms. Saint-Simon, for example, usually thought of the industrial employers as having a common interest with the workers against the old privileged classes of nobles, landowners and militarists. He recognized that in fact the employers were apt to treat the workers ill, but attributed this to their being caught up in a system based on the exploitation of *la classe la plus nombreuse et la plus pauvre*, and believed that if the privileged classes were overthrown, the technicians and administrators would act as the servants and not the masters of the people, becoming the *fonctionnaires* of the new industrial order. In order to ensure this, his followers wished to abolish inheritance of wealth and to make land and capital public property, to be entrusted to those persons who were capable of making the best use of it in the general interest. Fourier proposed to allow investors of capital a return on their investments in his projected *phalanstères* (associative communities), and did not envisage the advent of the new society as involving any struggle between capitalists and workers; but he also proposed to levy what amounted to a very stiff progressive tax on unearned incomes and contemplated that every worker would become in some measure an investing co-owner as well. Owen always expressed strong opposition to class-hatred: employers and capitalists, he said, were fellow victims with the workers of the bad, competitive system; and he called upon them to join hands with the workers in abolishing it. He was prepared to allow investors in his 'Villages of Co-operation' to receive a limited interest on their capital, but believed they would soon cease to claim it when the virtues of the new order had been proved in practice. As for the working employers, he expected them to be chosen by the workers as managers of the new co-operative establishments that were to replace capitalist enterprise. But Owen was as fully aware as any of the socialists of the actual exploitation of the workers and of the existence of class-antagonisms in capitalist society.

Where most of the early socialists differed from the Marxists who became the inspirers of later socialist movements was not in being unaware of class distinctions but in resting their case on arguments of justice and human brotherhood rather than on a conception of class-*power*. Marx's 'Scientific' Socialism was an attempt to demonstrate the certainty of the conquest of power by the working class quite apart from any consideration of what *ought* to happen, in a moral sense. Of course Marx, as much as any other socialist, believed class-exploitation, class-privilege, and class-monopoly to be morally bad, and wanted them to be swept away in the interests of human well-being. But he claimed that this was bound to occur, whether he wanted it or not, because of the inexorable movement of economic forces which were fundamentally independent of men's wills. This *was* his 'scientific' doctrine, resting on his materialist conception of history, which altogether excluded considerations of right and wrong. Marx believed in a natural law of social evolution which involved, as men's knowledge of productive techniques advanced, a growing 'socialization' of the processes of production. This, he held, carried with it a corresponding evolution in the field of human relations, destined to result in a complete democratization of economic affairs and in the achievement of a classless society. The way in which this must come about, he held, was the way of class-conflict, because no privileged class would ever yield up its superiority except under pressure from the class or classes it had been holding in subordination. Thus the progress of society from worse to better depended, not on appeals to goodwill or reason, but on the development of the power of the subjected class that stood next below the existing class of rulers. This conception of power as the key to the social problem did not mean that there were no moral issues at stake: it did mean that the moral aspect was irrelevant from the standpoint of predicting the course of events.

Herein lay indeed a sharp contrast; for all the 'Utopians' believed that, apart from considerations of power, it was possible to affect the future by appealing to reason and conscience. Among the 'Utopians', Saint-Simon had the keenest sense of historical development and was most clearly in the succession of the great eighteenth-century philosophers of the Enlightenment. For Saint-Simon, as for Condorcet and Turgot, the course of human history was essentially a matter of the progress of the human spirit – of the growth of reason, based on the growth of human knowledge. His language came near to Marx's at times, when he was proclaiming the advent of the industrial age and its corollary in the supersession of the old privileged orders by *les industriels*. But for Saint-Simon this process of historical evolution was a progress of the human mind – of scientific knowledge, including the knowledge of man himself: it was not a 'material' power external to man's will. It may be answered by Marxists that Marx also recognized the mind of man as a force in the making of history, as a part of the 'material' power which determined the course of development. But the emphasis was entirely different. Marx stressed the course of economic evolution as a natural force independent of men's wills (though not of their advance in knowledge, which was an essential part of the 'powers of production' as he defined them); whereas Saint-Simon stressed the progress of *les lumières* – of human enlightenment – as the essential formative force, which determined the character of the productive powers. Both men were determinists: both thought they could predict the future; but the one based his prediction on a belief in a law of evolution conceived in materialist terms, and the other on a law of the evolution of the mind of man.

This difference had important consequences. Saint-Simon and his followers thought the most important thing of all was the advancement and systematization of human knowledge, and that this would necessarily lead towards a society based on high production and distributive justice. The Marxists, on the other hand, thought that the main task was that of arousing the workers to a sense of their class-power, and that this would hasten the advent of the new classless society. Saint-Simon thought men were bound by a law of nature, to become more enlightened and that his efforts could only hasten and make more efficient a development that was bound to occur in any case. Marx thought that the evolution of the 'powers of production' was bound to carry the proletariat to victory, but that the victory could be hastened and made more efficient by stimulating the proletariat's confidence in its historic mission.

Most of the other 'Utopians' had much less historical sense than either Saint-Simon or Marx – though there were exceptions such as Constantin Pecqueur in France and J. F. Bray in England. Owen and Fourier, for example, both had a strong millennial tendency. Owen was apt to sweep up the entire past and present into a single heap, which he called the 'Old Immoral World' and contrasted with his 'New Society' – a society that could end human ills in a day if only men could be persuaded to establish it. Fourier, too, wrote as if all past ages up to his own had gone astray through a complete misunderstanding of human nature, which had only to be cleared up for the millennium to arrive at once. Marx was justly impatient at such unrealistic notions; and he was no less impatient at the unhistorical revolutionism of such socialists as Blanqui, who believed that the victory of the proletariat could be achieved by a *coup de main* of a handful of determined insurrectionists, without any need for a prior development of the proletariat's own sense of power and historic mission. Marx was essentially a political realist, who fought many battles with the unhistorical revolutionists as well as with the 'Utopians'.

No doubt he underestimated the time it would take for the proletariat to develop its organization and sense of power, and also the speed at which capitalism was advancing towards collapse because of its inherent 'contradictions'. But Marx, like Saint-Simon, had a keen sense of historical realism, even if his interpretations of the movement of historic forces were by no means always correct.

After 1848 the Marxist conception gradually conquered the greater part of the socialist movement. 'Utopianism' did not disappear; but the Utopians were driven away from the centre of the political stage and found refuge, for the most part, in the various forms of anarchism – particularly in the anarchist communism of Bakunin and Kropotkin. They came back – but with a significant difference – in the Syndicalist movements of France and Italy and in the Anarcho-Syndicalist movement of Spain. The difference was that, instead of working out models of perfect communities, the Syndicalists usually refused to offer any blue-prints of the future, and contented themselves with saying that when the state had been destroycd and the power of the workers established by 'direct action', the creative genius liberated by emancipation from class-oppression would speedily devise the right forms of social administration for the free communities of the new order. They accepted Marx's analysis of the problem in terms of class-power, but rejected power as the basis of the new free society which the victorious workers were to set up. They were 'Utopians' only in the sense that they believed the millennium would come in speedily when the capitalist system and its upholder, the state, had been over-thrown.

The Marxist version of socialism was fully proclaimed in 1848 in the *Communist Manifesto;* but it had little influence on the European revolutions of that year, and after their defeat socialism went for a time almost into eclipse. In Great Britain, Chartism slowly flickered out, despite Ernest Jones's efforts to recreate it on Marxian foundations during the 1850s: Paris, which had been the great centre of socialist ideas and movements, relapsed under Napoleon III into a quiescence partly accounted for by the dispersal in exile or prison of most of its leaders. Revival did not come, on any significant scale, till the

1860s: when it did come, Germany, rather than France, occupied for a time the leading position, with the followers of Marx and of Lassalle contending for the control of the developing working-class movement. In this contest the question of the socialist attitude to the state came to play a vitally important part. Marx regarded the capitalist state, which in Germany, and especially in Prussia, was also the semi-feudal state of the older privileged classes, as an enemy to be fought with and overthrown. Lassalle and his followers, on the other hand, looked on the state as a mechanism that could be transformed by the establishment of manhood suffrage into an instrument of social progress: they demanded that the state should place capital at the disposal of the organized workers for the establishment of free, co-operative productive enterprises. This was no new idea: it had been urged by many socialists in the 1830s and 1840s, and had been the central feature of Louis Blanc's policy of 'Organisation of Labour'. Marx had denounced it then, as running counter to the fundamental doctrine of class-struggle; and he denounced it again when it reappeared in Germany in the 1860s. German socialism came into being as a divided movement – the Lassallians *versus* the Marxist 'Eisenachers' led by August Bebel and Wilhelm Liebknecht – and the division persisted through the period during which Marx was attempting to rebuild on a new basis the international working-class revolutionary movement that had made its first abortive appearance in 1848.

Marx's instrument for this rebuilding was the First International – the International Working Men's Association which was founded in London in 1864. This was an amorphous body, centrally directed from London by a council made up largely of British trade unionists who sympathized with revolutions abroad without having any use for them at home, and for the rest of foreign exiles in London who were mostly prepared to accept Marx's leadership. The sections of the International which were founded in other countries, except Germany, were much less amenable to Marx's influence: the French section was dominated by followers of Proudhon, with a minority of Blanquists and only a sprinkling of Marxists: the Belgians, under César de Paepe, had their own line which was hostile to authoritarian policies: the Swiss were divided between German, French, and Russian influences: the Italians and the Spaniards were predominantly Anarchist, and looked for leadership to Bakunin rather than to Marx. The resolutions passed at the International's early congress were the outcome of a mixture of influences. Marx kept control of the central organization only because the British trade-union leaders, little interested in niceties of doctrine and regarding the whole affair as concerning mainly the Continental working classes, gave him, up to 1871, almost a free hand. Within the International there soon developed a bitter conflict between Marxists and Anarchists, with other tendencies playing only a secondary role.

Then came the Franco-Prussian War, the collapse of Napoleon's empire, and the proclamation of the shortlived Paris Commune. The Commune was a revolutionary outbreak in which outraged patriotism combined with a working-class revolutionism that harked back to the agitations of the thirties and forties and beyond them to the Jacobinism of 1793. The Paris Marxists took part in it, but were not strong enough to have the deciding voice. Marx himself had no share in inspiring it, and knew that it could not succeed. He rallied to its defence, in the famous manifesto on *The Civil War in France*, issued in the name of the International; but he knew that it would be the International's undoing. His British trade-union supporters, intent on their own attempts at peaceable reform and shocked at the events in France, dropped off one by one; and when the Commune had been quenched in blood by Thiers it was at Marx's own instance that the headquarters of the International were transferred from a Europe now too hot to hold it to New York. There, without effective leadership and remote from the movements it was supposed to co-ordinate and control, the International expired within a few years, as it was bound to do. Marx's second attempt to put himself at the head of a great international proletarian movement had ignominiously petered out. The Bakuninists, who had been driven out before the transfer to New York, held together for a time in a rump International of their own; but they soon ceased to command a wide following outside Spain and Italy.

Marxism did not, however, die after the fall of the Paris

Commune: it entered speedily on a new phase, which was in effect the birth of the social democratic movement. The establishment of the German Empire, with a Reichstag elected on a wide popular franchise, transformed the conditions of political action in Germany and made the division of the German socialists into two rival parties an unwarrantable barrier to electoral success, which the new franchise rendered for the first time possible. Under pressure of this electoral consideration Lassallians and Eisenachers patched up their quarrels, and in 1875 formed at Gotha a united German Social Democratic party; and this party became the model for the establishment of new socialist electoral parties in one Continental country after another. Up to that time the franchise had almost everywhere been so restricted as to give working-class parties practically no chance of electoral success. But after the British Reform Act of 1867, the German Constitution of 1870, and the establishment in France of the Third Republic, electoral rights were extended in other countries, and it became possible to organize socialist parties on a parliamentary basis, or rather with the contesting of parliamentary seats as one of their principal objectives. Such a policy was in practice as irreconcilable with the maintenance of Marx's attitude towards the existing state as it was with the Anarchism of Bakunin. In theory, it is no doubt possible for a working-class party to contest parliamentary elections without putting forward any projects of partial reform within the existing social and political order, and to use elections – and representatives, should any get elected on such terms – merely as means of propaganda for thoroughgoing socialism. In practice, such a line is possible only where the executive Government is entirely irresponsible to Parliament, and there is no chance of getting valuable reforms by parliamentary means. Such conditions existed in Russia after 1905; but they did not exist after the 1870s in France or even in Germany, or over most of Western Europe. In the West, the socialists could hope to get votes only if, in addition to their long-run socialist objectives, they put before the electors immediate programmes of reform within the existing political and economic system.

The German Social Democratic party of 1875, though it

largely adopted Marxism as a theoretical creed, in effect accepted this necessity, without which no fusion with the Lassallians would have been possible. Marx, sent by his German followers an advance copy of the proposed terms of fusion, protested angrily at what he described as a betrayal of socialist principle: his followers suppressed his long, argumentative protest, which was printed (as the *Critique of the Gotha Programme*) only many years after his death. He did not make his views public, realizing that the Eisenachers would repudiate him if he did. Social democracy was born as the outcome of a compromise of which the man generally regarded as its prophet violently disapproved.

What the Germans had done was not to repudiate Marx's doctrine of the class-struggle or his materialist conception of history but, while accepting these, to deny the conclusion he had drawn from them concerning the nature of the state and the appropriate political means of advancing from a capitalist to a socialist society. They had treated his view of the state as having been rendered obsolescent by the establishment of a wide franchise, and had set out to capture the state rather than to overthrow it utterly and put a new proletarian state in its place. The full consequences of the change appeared only gradually; and in Germany they were delayed by Bismarck's Anti-Socialist law of 1878, which forced the socialists back to underground activities. But with the repeal of this law in 1890 and the establishment of the right of organization and propaganda, the transformation of the party went on apace. At Erfurt, in 1891, it explicitly adopted, side by side with its ultimate programme, an immediate programme of social reform. Removing the Lassallian demand for state aid in the establishment of workers' co-operatives, and redrafting the economic part of its programme in such a way as to assert its entire loyalty to Marxism, the German Social Democratic party turned, as far as the still largely autocratic constitution of Germany (and still more of Prussia) would allow it, into a constitutional party commanding a wide following concerned mainly with reform rather than with revolution. Eduard Bernstein, in his famous attempt to procure a 'revision' of the Marxist doctrine in the late 1890s, wished to make the change explicit, at the cost of openly discarding a number of Marx's more disputable doctrines ('increasing misery' of the workers, impending collapse of capitalism through its own inner 'contradictions', and the sharp division of the whole people into contending classes of exploiters and exploited). He was defeated and reprimanded: but in practice the German Social Democratic party followed more and more closely the line he had recommended to it.

The social democratic parties in other countries which were modelled on the German original went largely the same way. In Russia, indeed, and in Russian Poland there emerged parties which maintained the older revolutionary tradition; but this involved a split, of which the rift between Bolsheviks and Mensheviks in Russia may serve as the outstanding example. In Great Britain Hyndman's Social Democratic Federation remained too weak ever to need to make a clear choice: it was superseded as a political electoral force in the 1890s by Keir Hardie's Independent Labour party. In France the social democrats (Jules Guesde's *Parti Ouvrier*) constituted only one element in a socialist political movement made up of a number of different tendencies – Blanquist, Proudhonist, Marxist, and others. The rival groups did not combine until 1905, and then only under the severe pressure of the turmoils arising out of the *affaire Dreyfus*. When they did unite, under the leadership of Jean Jaurès, their attitude to the state had much more in common with Lassalle's than with Marx's and the doctrine of outright hostility to the *bourgeois* state was sustained only by the Syndicalist *Confédération Générale du Travail*, which insisted on complete trade-union aloofness from parliamentary action. In Belgium, and also in Holland, right up to 1918 the maintenance of a narrow franchise restricted the socialist parties to a subordinate position in the Parliaments, and thus prevented them from developing mainly as electoral parties advocating programmes of immediate reforms. They were therefore able to go on talking the language of Marxism with less inconsistency than either the Germans or the French: but in the case of Belgium the close alliance between the Labour party, the trade unions, and the co-operative societies, as equal partners in a working-class alliance, made for a conception of socialism considerably different from that which found favour in Germany, where the political movement held the directing influence jealously in its own hands. In Italy, too, the extremely restricted franchise – up to 1913 – and the economic backwardness of the country prevented the development of an effective socialist party on the German model. Anarchism was strong in many of the country areas; and the socialist party led by Turati was weakened by the splitting away of a syndicalist wing, headed by the movement's leading theorist, Antonio Labriola. In Scandinavia, on the other hand, Sweden and Denmark developed parties closely modelled on the German, and these followed much the same course of development as essentially parliamentary bodies, 'revising' Marxism to fit the conditions of electoral activity.

Thus social democracy, which had begun as a revolutionary political movement based on a full acceptance of Marxist theory, turned under the influence of the franchise extension and the growth of parliamentary government more and more into a non-revolutionary agitation for reform and into an attempt to take over, instead of destroying, the machinery of the state. In Great Britain there was no corresponding development only because the climate of opinion among the workers was highly unfavourable to the reception of Marxian ideas. In almost all the continental countries organized religion was closely associated with political conservatism, and the working-class movements grew up in deep hostility to the churches. In Great Britain, on the other hand, nonconformist religion had a strong hold on the workers, as well as on the middle classes, and was traditionally associated with political liberalism. Nonconformity served for a considerable time as a force causing political labourism to develop inside the Liberal party, and served to prevent it from taking on any anti-religious character. Hyndman's Social Democratic Federation, which was anti-religious in the Continental manner, came up against a blank wall when it attempted to convert to socialism the main body of the British working class. The Independent Labour party was able to push it aside largely because, far from setting itself against religion, it set out to harness the ethical impulses associated with religion to the socialist cause. On such a basis there could be no acceptance of the materialist philosophy of Marxism, though, of course, some elements of the Marxist doctrine influenced Keir Hardie and his collaborators. In the hands of the Fabian Society and of the Independent Labour party and its successor, the Labour party, British socialism grew up as a non-Marxist demand for social justice, with the Sermon on the Mount, rather than *Das Kapital* or the *Communist Manifesto*, as its ultimate court of appeal.

There was, however, a second force at work in Great Britain; and this made on the whole for the same result. The conception of the course of history as determined finally by the forces of economic development was linked by Marx to the conception of the class-struggle as involving the revolutionary displacement of one governing class by another as the economic conditions became ripe. But an economic conception of history is equally reconcilable with an evolutionary, or gradualist, conception of social development. There is nothing contrary to logic in supposing that, as economic conditions change, political and social conditions change with them gradually, and not by revolutionary upheavel. Marx had dismissed this possibility, partly because of his Hegelian way of thought and partly because he held that no governing class would ever yield up its power without fighting its hardest to retain it. As against this view the Fabians, who also held a broadly economic conception of historical evolution, argued that under conditions of extended suffrage and responsible government the electorate could use its power to extract one concession after another from the ruling class, and to claim an increasing share in political authority for any representatives it chose to elect. Thus, they argued, the existing state could by a gradual process be transformed into a 'Welfare State', and a working-class party could be carried to political power by a sequence of electoral successes. This presupposed that the old governing class would not at any point decide to fight in arms in defence of its authority; and the Fabians held that in a parliamentary state enjoying responsible government it would in practice be very difficult for the governing class at any stage to defy the constitution. In the climate of British opinion, with its long tradition of responsible government and of gradual advance towards democratic control, this view seemed to fit the situation very much better than any more revolutionary theory – indeed, the evidently unrevolutionary attitude of the working class made any other notion untenable as a basis for mass political action.

Accordingly, British Labour and German Social Democracy had arrived, by the early years of the present century, at broadly the same conclusion, though they had travelled to it by widely different roads. The conditions of parliamentary campaigning under a wide franchise had, moreover, tended in both cases to establish in the minds of the party leaders a conception of democracy very different from Marx's. By the 'democracy' Marx meant the proletariat, and no one else. He assumed that the proletariat stood for the majority; but he thought in terms, not of majorities and minorities, but of *classes* contending for power. Under a parliamentary system, however, the factor that counts is the vote of the individual elector, to whatever class he belongs. A parliamentary socialist party cannot woo the proletariat alone: it has to get all the votes it can, from any source; and its leaders therefore think instinctively in terms not of classes but of majorities and minorities of individual voters. They are led to accept a conception of 'democracy', as meaning majority rule, which is entirely at variance with Marx's conception of it as class-rule. Thus socialism, which in its early Marxian period had espoused the notion of the coming 'dictatorship of the proletariat', reverted later in the west of Europe, as the conditions of political action changed, to a conception much more closely akin to that of the 'Utopian' Socialists whose attitude I have discussed earlier in this essay. They were appealing, not to a single class – even if they did look to the workers for the bulk of their support – but to all persons of goodwill, and were appealing on grounds of ethics and justice, rather than as the exponents of a 'scientific' doctrine of inevitability and 'historic mission'.

Modern communism began as a return to the older Marxist tradition. Or rather, as it began in Russia, it continued that tradition unbroken. In Russia – indeed, over most of eastern Europe – nothing had happened to throw doubt on Marx's analysis, based as it was on the conditions of the first half of the nineteenth century in the West. In Russia, what capitalist enterprise there was grossly exploited the workers, and the state, still in the hands of a feudal autocracy, stood ready to break and bludgeon, to banish and at need to shoot down, any who rebelled. The tradition of the socialist movement was made up of secret conspiracy, of espionage and betrayal, of revolt brutally suppressed, and, after 1905, of actual revolution. Behind the existing movement, which was sharply divided, lay a long history of doctrinal conflict – above all, of disputes between 'Westernizing' Marxists and those who believed that Russia must make a native socialism, resting on the peasant rather than on the relatively few industrial workers. Both factions were further divided – the Social Revolutionaries into a left wing with a tradition of assassination and violence and a right wing which aimed at uplifting the peasants through land reform, education, and co-operation; the 'Westernizers' into a left wing which aimed straight at revolution under socialist leadership and a right wing which held that the country must first achieve the liberal republic and pass through the successive stages of capitalist development before it could become ripe for socialism. Right up to 1917 the Social Revolutionaries – the agrarian socialists – greatly outnumbered the Social Democrats, Bolsheviks, and Mensheviks together; but the Social Democrats had behind them the bulk of the most cohesive group – the factory workers and miners and oil-field workers. The Bolshevik section had also the advantage of possessing the one really brilliant leader, Lenin, and the most disciplined party organization, inured to the need for cohesion by years of secret agitation.

The Social Revolutionaries had much in common with the anarchists everywhere. They were localizers, believers in spontaneous action, distrustful of disciplined leadership and organization. As the revolution had to face the immense difficulties of sheer disintegration due to the war, the Social Revolutionaries went down like ninepins before Bolshevik discipline and ruthless courage. So did the Mensheviks, swept aside with the weak *bourgeoisie* whom they had hoped to make the instruments of the transition through capitalism to a socialism of the Western type. The Bolsheviks remained, to reinterpret in action the Marxism of 1848, which fitted the conditions of

contemporary Russia a great deal better than the social democracy that had replaced it in the more advanced countries of
Western Europe.

The Leninist Marxism which emerged during the early years
of the Bolshevik régime was, in a literal sense, faithful in almost
every particular – save one – to Marx's doctrine. The one
outstanding difference was that Lenin revised Marx's theory
by asserting that it was possible for the proletariat, instead of
first helping the *bourgeoisie* into power and then turning upon
them after their victory, to take power at once and carry through
the necessary process of capitalist development under proletarian control. This was Lenin's theory of 'state capitalism',
and it was definitely a departure from what Marx had held.
Besides this, there was a more subtle difference. Marx had
spoken of the 'dictatorship of the proletariat' as a necessary
stage in the transition to a classless society. But he had never
explained very clearly what he meant, except that the workers
were to destroy the old state of the exploiters and set up a new
one in its place. Lenin, however, made the 'dictatorship' the
very corner-stone of his theory, and interpreted it as signifying
in effect the dictatorship of the Communist party as the only
true representative of the proletariat and the only interpreter
of its historic mission. The role of the 'party', merely adum-
brated in certain passages of the *Communist Manifesto*, was
worked up into a complete theory of class-leadership. Lenin
always insisted that the party must so act as to carry the mass
sentiment of the workers – including the poorer peasants –
along with it: it was to 'dictate', not *to* the workers, but on
their behalf. But the one thing led easily to the other. If the
'party' alone had a correct understanding of the processes
of historical evolution and of the workers' part in them, it
alone was in a position to tell the workers what to do in their
own interest. According to Marx's determinist doctrine there
could be only one right course, marked out by the development
of the economic forces. Accordingly there had to be a central
determination of party policy to ensure that this one right
course should be followed. 'Democratic centralism', the laying
down at the centre, after debate within the party, of a line which
every party member must accept without further question,

logically followed. The party became a dictatorship over the workers, and, within the party, the structure became more and more hierarchical and the determination of policy, under stress of continual danger to the régime, more and more a matter for the central leadership. Purges and convictions of 'deviationists' followed as a necessary sequel; when once the party leadership had decided a thing, all questioning of it came to be regarded as treason to the working class.

Most of these developments of communist theory came only after Lenin's death. They were largely the work of Stalin, who had not, like Lenin, any understanding of Western socialism. Lenin, as an old Bolshevik, had been essentially a 'Westernizer', looking to the industrial proletariat to be the principal agent for lifting Russia out of its primitive backwardness. Stalin, too, wanted to push on with industrialization, as a means of defence against Western capitalism; but in his eyes the West had nothing to teach the Russians except in the technological field. In his essential ideas Stalin remained Eastern; and under his influence Marxism was transformed into an oriental doctrine, untinged with any respect for the cultural, as distinct from the purely technological, achievements of the West. By a strange paradox, that very Slavophil attitude which, earlier, the Russian Social Democrats had denounced as the cardinal error of their Narodnik and Social Revolutionary rivals came back as the creed of triumphant communism – until, presently, it had to be believed that every important scientific and technological discovery had really been due to a Russian, and that out of the West had come nothing except imperialism and exploitation.

This thoroughgoing 'revision' of Marxist doctrine was, of course, greatly fostered by Western mishandling of the new Russia, both between the two world wars and after 1945. The countries of Western Europe did their best between the wars to wreck the Soviet Union or to treat it as a pariah; and after 1945, when Western Europe was too weak to continue along the same lines, anti-communist hysteria took a strong hold on the United States, powerfully reinforcing the bent of Stalinism, already strong enough, towards the isolation of the Soviet peoples from contact with Western movements and ideas. There were attempts after 1918 to rebuild a united Socialist

International, broad enough to comprehend both communists and Western social democratic and labour parties – and parallel attempts to create a comprehensive Trade Union International. On the trade union side, these efforts were resumed after 1945, with temporary apparent success. But neither between the wars nor after 1945 was there ever any real prospect of a united movement. Even in Lenin's day the ideas of the two kinds of socialism were much too far apart; and with Stalin's advent to power the last vestige of a common outlook disappeared. The Western parties and trade unions had fully accepted the policy of constitutional action, of a gradual capture of the state, and meantime of its use as an agent of social welfare, and of ballot-box democracy as the only legitimate road of advance towards a socialist society. The Soviet party and its satellites, on the other hand, believed in the necessity of world revolution, in the impending downfall of capitalist society because of its inner contradictions, and in a one-party system which had nothing in common with the multi-party systems of the Western countries. There was no bridging such gulfs.

How came it, then, that the communists were able to find powerful working-class support in certain of the Western countries – above all, in France, as well as in Italy, and, between the wars, up to the Nazi *coup*, in Germany? The answer is that, in these countries, the processes of ballot-box democracy, after carrying the social democrats a certain distance along the road to electoral success, showed no signs of carrying them on farther to the actual conquest of political power. Socialist propaganda and organization could win over a large minority of the population, not a majority – much less a stable majority to serve as the basis for a thorough refashioning of the economic and social system. Only in Great Britain and in Scandinavia did the socialists reach a strong enough electoral position even to hold independent office for any length of time; and in these countries communism remained weak. Elsewhere socialists could only oppose, or take part in coalitions of which it was an implied condition that the basis of the social system must not be changed. A large section of the working classes accordingly gravitated towards communism, which at least held out the hope of accomplishing by revolution, with the Soviet Union's aid, the great social transformation that seemed to be quite beyond the reach of the constitutional socialist parties.

There were, of course, additional factors at work. In France, in Germany, and in Italy class antagonisms went very much deeper than in Great Britain or Scandinavia, or, for that matter, the United States. Germany, up to 1918, had never been a fully constitutional state; and the attempt to make it one, under the Weimar Republic, born in defeat and faced throughout with appalling difficulties, was never a success. In Italy parliamentary government had never been more than a façade, and a wide suffrage had been conceded only in 1913, just before the First World War. In both these countries fascism, directed against socialism and liberalism in all their forms, engendered communism as a counter-movement. In France, where parliamentary government had been more of a reality, the welfare state had signally failed to develop after 1918, and the strong syndicalist tradition of the trade unions, with its emphasis on class-war and opposition to the *bourgeois* state, was much more closely akin, despite its anarchist element, to communism than to Western social democracy. Thus Russian communism, despite its growingly oriental temper, continued to find allies in the heart of the West – allies strong enough to thwart the hopes of social democrats, but not to win power on their own account.

All this amounts to saying that the socialist movement, which began as an idealistic drive for social justice and for co-operation, instead of competition, as the right foundation for human relations in the new era ushered in by the great French Revolution, has today become divided into two separate movements, resting on deeply antagonistic philosophies. This divorce was heralded by Marx, when he set out to establish a new 'Scientific Socialism' based on the concept of class-power. But Western Marxism, under the conditions of political and economic development in the advanced capitalist countries during the second half of the nineteenth century, lost much of its revolutionary character, and therewith reverted more and more to ethical appeals for social justice, even while its votaries continued to recite the Marxist slogans of class-war. The revival of the older Marxism occurred, not primarily in the West, but in those parts of Europe to which Marx's diagnosis continued to apply because of their economic backwardness and of the starker conditions of class-antagonism which went with it. From these backward countries the older Marxism – with a difference due to its change of habitat – streamed back into the West between the wars as the difficulties of Western capitalism multiplied, and as stalemate, or worse, overtook the leading social democratic parties of continental Europe. For a moment, in 1945, it looked as if, under the leadership of the victorious British Labour party, the Western social democratic parties might be able so to rally their forces as to sweep their political antagonists, largely tainted as they were with war-time 'collaboration', from the field, and to establish in the Western countries the foundations of a democratic parliamentary socialist régime. But British Labour was neither alive enough to the possibilities nor internationally minded enough to give the required lead; and the possibility of a victorious socialist 'Third Force' in world affairs, if it ever existed, speedily disappeared. The social democrats of France and Italy were reduced to a role of opposition, weakened by the desertion of most of their followers to communism or near-communism; and in western Germany, though stronger, they were not strong enough to win an electoral majority. It began to look as if, as a great international force, social democracy had shot its bolt, despite its sustained strength in Great Britain and in the Scandinavian countries.

Moreover, after the Second World War, socialism ceased to be, as it had been previously, an essentially European movement, with no more than outposts elsewhere. The rising tide of nationalism in Asia and in the colonial territories of the European powers in other continents fitted in much more easily with communism than with parliamentary socialism, which was a creed devised to fit the conditions of advanced countries possessing responsible government. The communists set out everywhere to exploit to the full the discontents of the nationalist movements, by denouncing the imperialist practices of the capitalist countries communism gained the day in China, and troubled the British, the French, and the Americans (in Korea)

with colonial wars which dissipated their resources. Communism was a ready article for export to a great many countries
for which parliamentary socialism had no message the main
body of the people could even begin to understand. Indeed,
the parliamentary socialists, forced on to the defensive, found
themselves the reluctant allies of their political opponents in a
reliance on American aid which involved their enlistment in a
world-struggle between the world's two remaining great powers
– the United States and the Soviet Union – a struggle in which
the issue was primarily between capitalism and communism,
with social democracy as third man out.

Yet communism, even if it be a necessary stage in the transition from capitalism to a new social order in Eastern Europe, in
China, and in other countries in which effective reconstruction
of society can hardly begin without a revolutionary change, is
manifestly inappropriate to the needs either of the United States
or of the advanced countries of Western Europe. These countries
have far too complicated a class-structure for the simple class-
theory of the *Communist Manifesto* to fit their conditions, or
for their peoples to want thoroughgoing revolution on a class
basis as a means to change. Communism will not prevail in
Western Europe unless the Russians install it by sheer force in
war: it cannot under any conditions prevail in the United States.
The communist *World* Revolution is not going to happen:
it cannot happen in face of American immunity to its appeal.
In the West except as an outcome of war, capitalism cannot
be replaced except by some form of social democracy; and if
social democracy is too weak to replace it, the continuance of
capitalism, however it may be modified in secondary respects,
is assured for a long time to come. It shows no sign of speedy
collapse under pressure of its own 'contradictions' – such as
Marx, and later Lenin, expected to occur.

Socialism, then, is no longer a single movement, making in a
single direction. In the West it is – as the first forms of socialism
were – fundamentally a drive towards social justice and equality,
rather than a class quest for power. It can, of course, no more
avoid having to think in terms of power as well as of morals
than communism, for all its insistence on the factor of power,
can avoid invoking the aid of ethical appeals. The communist

needs to feel that his cause is righteous, as well as historically determined: the Western socialist needs to feel that the workers are behind him, as well as that his cause is good. Both are aiming, in a sense, at the same thing – a classless society – and both believe in collective action as the means of advancing towards it. Both regard private property in the essential instruments of production as inconsistent with the absence of class distinctions: both in some sense want to 'socialize' men's minds by socializing their environment. But whereas the communist seeks these ends by means of class action and regards the dictatorship of a class as a necessary step towards their attainment, the Western socialist looks to the winning of an electoral majority, however composed, and repudiates dictatorship as inconsistent with his conception of the democratic principle. Western socialism acts on the assumption of a basic social solidarity which holds the community together: communism denies this solidarity in any society which has not been through its social revolution and eliminated feudal and capitalist privilege. The two conceptions are related to two different kinds of society. In Great Britain, as in the United States, in Switzerland, in Scandinavia, in Canada and Australia, and to a less extent in Belgium and Holland, this underlying social solidarity is a fact based on a long historical experience. Even in France and in Germany the same tradition exists, though it is partly counteracted by other factors. But in Russia and over most of Eastern Europe this solidarity has not existed in the past, and is barely intelligible to those whose thinking is based on the history of these countries. Accordingly, the conception of an overriding class loyalty, transcending national loyalty, meets with no such obstacles in Eastern as in Western Europe; and a socialism that dismisses nationalism (except when it is being exploited as a means of stimulating 'anti-imperialist' revolt) as a petty *bourgeois* concept is able to make its realistic way. What has still to be seen is what will happen in the long run in those parts of the world in which communism and nationalism are now appearing as uneasy allies.

Nationalism and the sense of social solidarity are, however, by no means necessarily the same. Nationalism can be, and often is, the creed of a group or class within a nation, rather than of the nation as a whole. Marx spoke of it as if he supposed it was always of this limited kind, because his entire philosophy involved treating every concept as in the last resort a class-concept. It is of course true that in class-ridden societies the ruling classes often identify themselves with the nation; and Marx was in fact largely right about the nationalist movements of his own day – though not wholly so in relation to France, where the revolutionary tradition of national unity was strong. But there can exist, without a nationalist movement in a political sense, an attitude of social solidarity permeating a whole people, or at any rate cutting right across class-differences, in such a way as to limit very greatly the possibilities of fundamental class-conflict. Such a sentiment can exist, I think, only in societies which are either very static, so that habit suffices to hold them together, or very mobile, so that the classes they contain are continually shifting both in their nature and in respect of the individuals composing them. In the former type of society everyone has his station and knows it: in the latter, even if class is still a prominent category, status is no longer definite or unchangeable, and does not mark men off into sharply separated groups. It is in the intermediate types of society, in which there is a conflict between a static and a mobile sector, that the sense of social solidarity is least likely to be strong.

Such a conflict exists to a great extent in those economically backward countries which have been recently subjected to the impact of industrialism. As long as this impact remains mainly foreign it gives rise to forms of nationalist rejection of the foreigner which create a sentiment of union; but as soon as the forces of change come to be largely internal – through the development of native capitalism, native trade unionism, and so on – this unity tends to disappear, not being rooted in any deep social solidarity but simply in hostility to foreign influence. The communist leaders are aware of this: they realize that, in taking sides with 'nationalism' directed against foreign influence, they are helping to create the conditions in which national unity will give place to class-conflict as the mobile elements in the societies concerned are brought into direct conflict with the static elements and as this conflict in turn is replaced with the victory of the former, by a conflict between capitalist and worker. This is almost exactly how Marx envisaged the situation in the 1840s, except that he was then dealing mainly with a state of affairs in which there were no longer in Western Europe (except in Italy) serious problems of foreign domination to be faced. There had been, however, quite recently such problems in Germany and elsewhere during the period of Napoleon's European supremacy.

Social democratic thought cannot grapple easily with problems of this order, because it is an emanation of liberalism, based on the conditions of countries in which the static elements in the social structure have had to give way to the mobile elements – in other words, where capitalism has already subordinated the feudal elements to its own needs. Paradoxically, it is precisely in those countries in which *bourgeoisie* and *proletariat* are most free to fight each other and have least need to combine in order to fight against aristocratic privilege that these contending classes are least disposed to push their quarrel to extremes, because, far from becoming more uniform, they become more diverse and interpenetrated. But this state of affairs exists in a high degree only in a very limited number of countries; and I am afraid the conclusion has to be that the social democratic form of socialism is for the present of equally limited applicability in the world. It is not applicable to countries in which a fundamental revolution – for example, in the land system – is a necessary starting-point for real social change: nor is it applicable after such a revolution until there has been time for the post-revolutionary settlement to have become stabilized and generally accepted, so that the dominance of power-considerations which is a necessary accompaniment of revolution can wear off. Only stable societies possessing a sense of solidarity can in practice give ethical factors priority over considerations of power.

This essay is an attempt to answer the question 'What is socialism?' in terms of the present day. It contains nothing that even pretends to be a definition of socialism, either as it exists today or in the light of its history. Socialism cannot be defined in a sentence or a paragraph because it is fundamentally not a system but a movement which has taken, and will doubtless continue to take, diverse forms both from country to country and under the influence of particular theorists and practical exponents. It can be, up to a point, described and characterized, but not defined. Thus, one essential element in it is the stress laid on the need for collective regulation of social and economic affairs, and therewith its rejection of the entire philosophy of *laissez-faire*. But socialism is not alone in rejecting *laissez-faire;* there are plenty of 'plannists' who are among its most violent opponents. A second element is its thoroughgoing hostility to class-divisions and its aspiration towards a 'class-less society'. This it shares with the anarchists and syndicalists, but, I think, with no one else, though there is, of course, a kind of radical individualism that is sometimes allied with it in the struggle against 'class-privilege'. Thirdly, socialism traditionally stands for 'democracy'; but democracy can be conceived of in so many different ways that the word, by itself, is not of much help. It does, however, provide the necessary clue to the deep division that exists today between communism and the socialism of the Western countries. For communism, the class itself is the unit in terms of which all political structures are to be assessed; and accordingly democracy is the rule of a class – of the working class as the representative champion of the unprivileged. For Western socialists, on the other hand, the individual is the final repository of ethical values, and democracy involves majority rule coupled with respect for individual rights. Western socialism, in the last analysis, is 'Utopian' rather than 'Scientific'. It is conceived of as a means to the good life for the individuals who make up human societies, and not as a destined outcome of a predetermined historical evolution that lies outside the individual's control.

Democratism

RICHARD ARTHUR WOLLHEIM

Richard Wollheim was born in 1923 and educated at Balliol College, Oxford. Since 1963 he has been Grote Professor of Philosophy of Mind and Logic in the University of London.

His publications include: *F. H. Bradley*, 1959; *Socialism and Culture*, 1961; *On Drawing an Object* (inaugural lecture), 1965; *Art and Its Objects*, 1968; *Freud*, 1971; *On Art and the Mind* (essays and lectures), 1973; *Freud, a collection of critical essays*, 1974.

Democracy

Richard Wollheim

I

The Ancient Greeks are generally regarded as the founders of
democracy. And rightly so, for it is to them that we are indebted
for the earliest examples of democracy in practice and in theory,
and indeed for the word itself.

It needs to be remembered, however, that, ultimately, antiquity rejected democracy.[1] As a form of government it lacked
permanence even in Athens, and in the realm of speculation,
the most famous thinkers both of Greece and Rome – Plato
and Aristotle, Cicero and Seneca – were against it. One consequence of this is that our knowledge and understanding of
classical democratic thought is of necessity partial and limited;
and some of its finest expressions – such as the Funeral Oration
of Pericles – have been influential more through successive mis-
interpretations than in virtue of what they actually say.

Both the practice and the theory of democracy appear to be
somewhat older than the word itself. It is convenient to regard
Cleisthenes as the creator of Athenian democratic government
(c. 508 B.C.), but it is most unlikely that either he or his contem-
poraries used the term $\delta\eta\mu\omega\kappa\rho\alpha\tau\iota\alpha$.[2] Equally, it seems that many
of the arguments later to be used in favour of democracy had
already been voiced in an earlier controversy: that between the
supporters of the unfettered rule of one man and those who believed in a system under which all were equal before the law
($\iota\sigma\omega\nu\omega\mu\iota\alpha$).[3] This controversy we glimpse in the works of Aeschy-
lus (*Pers.* 213–4; *Pr. Bound* 323–4; *Suppliants, passim*) and,
more liberally, in the famous account given by Herodotus
(*Hist.* III 80–4) of a debate between a number of Persian nobles
immediately upon the death of the Magian usurper in 522 B.C.
They discuss what kind of government should be adopted, and
in the course of the debate – which though clearly apocryphal as
a piece of Persian history is most probably a good index of
'progressive' Athenian thought of the period just after the

Persian War (491–479 B.C.) – Otanes, the supporter of ἰσονομια, not merely puts forward what are to be the main democratic arguments but also lays down the terms within which most future discussion of the subject is to be contained. These deserve examination:

In the first place, the discussion about democracy is primarily a discussion about forms of government, not one about forms of society. Of course, it was a commonplace of Greek political thinking that constitutional forms have an all-important effect on the manners or ways (τρόποι) of the citizens. So, for instance, Pericles in the Funeral Oration (Thuc. *Hist*. II. 35–46) claims that Athenian democracy was an education for all its members; and Plato, in asserting a complete parallelism between the organization of a Polis and the organization of the souls of those who live in it, was only generalizing popular conceptions. But, for all that, democracy was not associated in the classical mind with any clear-cut form of society in the sense of specific social structure. To Pericles, for instance, democracy is perfectly compatible with differences of wealth; what it is not compatible with is that these differences should carry with them any political influence. In Demosthenes' Fourth Philippic (*Orationes* X. 44) we find the same conception. Even Aristotle, the most sociologically minded of ancient thinkers, who talks of democracy as the natural product of a particular form of society (*Pol*. III. 1286b), has yet nothing serious to say about it as an active agent in society. Moreover it must be remembered that the advocates of democracy (with the exception of a few radical sophists, e.g. Antiphon) regarded it as perfectly consistent with the exclusion of slaves, foreigners, and women from political life; and even, it would seem, with an oppressive régime over subject territory (cf. Pericles' Funeral Oration).

Secondly, democracy as a form of government is rigorously connected with, if not identified by, certain specific political institutions. Otanes refers to the selection of officials by lot, the scrutiny at the end of a term of office, and the decision of policy by popular assembly. In practice democrats recognized that certain offices of state, e.g. the command of the army, called for special skill and in consequence were prepared to allow that such posts should be removed from the sphere of lottery. But apart from this and similar minor modifications, the list of essential democratic institutions remains fairly constant throughout the classical period.

Thirdly, the superiority or otherwise of forms of government is to be determined by a criterion that is, after all, essentially *practical* – if in the very highest sense of the word; namely, the capacity to provide rational and harmonious government, both rationality and harmony being conceived of as empirically verifiable phenomena. As an application of this criterion the superiority of democracy is held to rest on the surer wisdom of the many. Those to whom democracy gives power may individually vary in intelligence and goodwill, but collectively they are bound to be superior. This view which is suggested by Otanes reappears in the Funeral Oration, though its classical formulation is in Aristotle (*Pol.* III. 1281b) who, however, recounts it more as a good and established argument than as one that he personally accepts. Behind this argument there lies the great issue in Greek political philosophy: whether government is an expert skill, like medicine and navigation, or a matter in which all are equally competent. This issue finds its most philosophical expression in the *Republic*, where the argument is between government based on mere Opinion (δόξα), which is the possession of the many, and government grounded in Truth (ἀληθεία), which is the prerogative of the few. Plato claims to 'prove' the superiority of philosophical rule, and democracy is in consequence condemned.

Neither of two famous modern arguments for democracy – i.e., the moral argument that all men have the right to govern themselves, and the sceptical argument that since men can never know what is right, they should be governed in accordance with their wishes – is much heard of as far as we know in antiquity. Aristotle at one point mentions one established 'democratic' argument which might seem to have a sceptical ring – i.e., that 'the diner, not the cook, will be the best judge of a feast' (*Pol.* 1282a). However, Aristotle in this passage is not maintaining that there is no certain method of judging good government, but rather is suggesting that hitherto this method may have been misconceived.

In classical thought – and so ultimately in later thought based directly upon it – democracy is seldom considered in isolation. Constitutional discussion generally takes the form of drawing up a list of all possible forms of government and then contrasting, favourably or unfavourably, the merits of each with each. Not only do different thinkers vary in their estimates of democracy, but they tend to disagree on the meaning that they attach to the concept according to the way they have drawn up their initial lists. For the list being intended as exhaustive, each item in it draws its meaning negatively from the other items, i.e., it means what they don't mean. In the *Republic* the classification of states (i.e., imperfect states) is fourfold – timocracy, oligarchy, democracy, tyranny; in Xenophon's *Memorabilia* it is fivefold – kingship, tyranny, aristocracy, plutocracy, democracy; in the *Politicus* it is sixfold – kingship, aristocracy and democracy by consent, and tyranny, oligarchy and democracy by violence; in the *Politics* it is again sixfold – kingship, aristocracy and polity, and tyranny, oligarchy and democracy. This rather sterile method of discussing government – as though all possible forms of organization were timelessly laid open to inspection and History had nothing to teach – was unfortunately the feature of classical speculation that medieval thinkers found easiest to assimilate. In consequence it disfigures much of their speculation. Significantly, however, the real and permanent contribution of the Middle Ages to the history of democracy was made in the field not of theory but of practice: in the development of representation. Representational institutions, though not unknown in antiquity – as some historians have claimed – were nearly everywhere of far less importance than the 'primary assemblies' in which all the citizens participated.[4]

II

The development of the concept of democracy in Anglo-American discussions is hard to trace. In the first place, it is extremely complex. Secondly, it is intertwined with the history of related concepts such as equality, liberty, toleration, etc.; to separate them out is almost impossible, to leave them involved is disastrous. And thirdly, there is no clear dividing line between the history of democracy and the present condition of democracy with all the problems and controversies that surround it. Accordingly, the best that can be done is to isolate the most important single incidents in this long history.

1. THE PURITANS. It was in the course of the English Civil War, amongst the more militant Puritan sects, that the modern notion of democracy originated. It was the product of two dominant ideas of Puritanism. First, the belief in the separation of church and state. The original Calvinist doctrine of passive obedience gave way under the impact of official hostility and persecution to a vociferous separatism. This made possible for the first time in modern history a purely secular political theory. Secondly, there was the belief in 'the priesthood of all believers'. According to this doctrine, man should be left free to follow his own vocation, and in doing so he stood in no need of the mediation of either priest or presbyter. Transposed into political terms the idea of freedom meant that man had no obligation to any government that sought to control him for anything but his own benefit, and the idea of self-sufficiency meant that man had no need of any government that sought to control him for his own benefit – he could do that for himself. These views, which are particularly associated with the Levellers (John Lilburne, John Wildman, Overton and Walwyn) crystallized in the course of the long discussions on the type of constitution that England was to have after the Civil War, and they received their most specific formulation in the Agreement of the People presented at the Putney Debates (Nov.–Dec. 1647).[5]

The central thesis of Puritan democracy is that the basis of all legitimate government is *consent*. But this notion of consent suffers gradual dilution the closer the argument comes to practical politics. At its most extreme it means that everyone should consent to every single law that commands his obligation – a view which leads to what might be called the 'market' view of democracy as a permanently functioning mechanism for registering the popular will: more moderately the notion means that everyone should consent to those who make laws for him, while at its weakest it is held to involve no more than that everyone should 'have a voice in electing'.

2. THE REVOLUTION OF 1688. The next stage in the history of democracy is recorded in John Locke's *Second Treatise of Civil Government* (1689), a document which has always been regarded as a justification of the Glorious Revolution of 1688 though it was probably written and its leading ideas certainly laid down some years before. Here the political theory of the Puritans is taken up but with its revolutionary implications neutralized. The 'birthright' of every English citizen, on which the Levellers had insisted, is exchanged for a fixed list of 'natural rights'. Significantly, these rights do not include any specifically political rights, i.e., rights to exercise or control political power. Natural rights give man only what might be called an indirect interest in government, in that the government is responsible for safeguarding these natural rights. This responsibility is expressed in Locke's *Treatise* by means of the old metaphor of a *social contract* to which the people and the government are the two parties; the people pledge their obligation to the government and in return the government undertakes to protect the people's rights. If the government fails to keep its side of the contract the people automatically can revoke theirs. In other words, the right of everyone to a share in the government on which the Puritans had laid such stress has now been whittled down to no more than the right to revolt against the government if things go too far.

3. THE AMERICAN REVOLUTION. The prevailing theory of the American Revolution is Lockean. Both Jefferson and Madison explicitly declared themselves to be democrats – though at this period the 'democratic form of government' and the 'republican form of government' seem to have been used as synonyms. Democracy, however, is to be contrasted not so much with other and specific types of government, as with any kind of arbitrary or tyrannical rule. To Madison the real danger is 'the spirit of faction', i.e., the spirit that leads one part of the community to try and rule the rest in its own sectional interests, and he welcomed representation in some form or another as a good method of curbing this spirit. However, it was not the only method, nor even a particularly sacrosanct method. For it had in the first place to be supplemented by a series of constitutional

checks and balances; and secondly, it introduced dangers of its
own – in Madison we hear for the first time of the 'tyranny of
the majority'.

Amongst the American revolutionaries there was also a more
radical democratic theory.[6] This finds classical expression in
Tom Paine's *Common Sense* (1776). Paine believed that all
government was an evil, but that it could be a justified evil. To
be justified it had to concur with the will of the majority, and
Paine supported representation as the method of assuring that
it did so. Paine's significance in the history of democratic thought
is twofold. In the first place – as he himself said of the French
Revolution – he 'grafted representation upon democracy'.
Prior to Paine there had been a tendency on the part of more
radical thinkers to regard representation with suspicion as mask-
ing the true expression of popular consent, whereas it was the
more conservatively minded thinkers who welcomed it, at any
rate in a modified form, as one of the various elements in a
'balanced' constitution. Secondly, in Paine we see the growing
awareness that democracy involves a great deal in the way of
social reform and economic redistribution.

Despite the support that the more radical democrats received
in, for example, Massachusetts and Pennsylvania, they were unsuccessful in their programme, and even their political objectives
were unrealized.

4. THE UTILITARIANS. The Utilitarian democratic theory is the
product of two general principles – one psychological, the other
moral – both of which derive directly from the thought of the
Enlightenment. The first principle is that all men pursue their
own happiness. The second is that the only justification of any
action is that, compared with alternatives, it produces the greatest happiness of the greatest number. From the first principle it
follows that some government is necessary; from a combination
of the two principles it follows that democracy is the best form
of government. For if everyone pursues his own happiness and
government ought to pursue the happiness of the greatest
number, then government must be in the hands of the greatest
number. Democracy is no longer claimed as a right – Bentham
dismissed the doctrine of Natural Rights as 'a pomposity on

stilts' – but is advocated as the only possible means to a self-evidently desirable end.

It is indicative of the Utilitarians' detached scientific attitude to forms of government that the early Utilitarians avoided the democratic conclusion from their premises, either because they believed in the natural harmony of interests (a belief popularized by the political economists of the day), or because they believed that properly trained intellectuals might by their superior intelligence transcend the ordinary egotistic condition of humanity and act as altruistic legislators. It seems that it was James Mill who converted Bentham to democratic beliefs,[7] and certainly the best statement of the position of democratic Utilitarianism or Philosophical Radicalism is his *Essay on Government* (1820). Even he, however, advocates not universal suffrage but only a suffrage wide enough to secure the representation of all interests and to make the predominance of sinister interests impossible.

5. THE STRUGGLE FOR MAJORITY RULE. In America the struggle for democracy – in the fullest sense of unqualified rule by the majority – was resumed in the early part of the nineteenth century. The debates in the Massachusetts Convention of 1820, the New York Convention of 1821, and the Virginia Convention of 1829–30, the prolonged controversy in South Carolina, and the bitter struggle in Rhode Island culminating in the 'Dorr War' of 1842, mark the various phases in the struggle of limited v. universal suffrage. The arguments of the conservatives vary: sometimes they appeal to a view of government as a balance of interests, sometimes to the rights of property, sometimes to fears of majority tyranny, sometimes to the absurdity of general political principles and rights, sometimes to local circumstances. By comparison the reformers are of one voice. To them it seemed absurd to concede suffrage *to a certain extent* and then stop; any good reason one had for going so far, was a reason for going further, for wherever one drew the line must be arbitrary. Gradually the logic of this position triumphed.

In Great Britain the position was different. The constitution not being in the first place an artefact, the creature of debate and choice, there was no original *ratio decidendi* to which appeal could be made. In consequence each time the suffrage was extended – in 1832, in 1867, and in 1884 – the liberals tended to stress the practical necessity of the measure, while the conservatives emphasized its practical dangers. On neither side do we find much theoretical discussion apart from John Stuart Mill's *Representative Government* (1861) which combined Utilitarianism with a profound sense of minority rights.

The peculiar contribution of Great Britain to the spread of democracy consisted not so much in any theoretical justification of the extension of the suffrage as in practical measures for making this extension effective. The history of this consists of two distinct processes. The first process was the growing dependence of government upon the representative assembly. This meant on the one hand that no government could survive without a majority in, or at any rate the confidence of, the House of Commons, and secondly that it was not enough for the government to present and defend its policy before the House of Lords.[8] The second process was the gradual development of party organization. In its modern form this dates from the 1830s, but the vital event is the formation of the Birmingham 'Caucus' after 1867.[9] For all its possible drawbacks, the development of political parties has had a threefold significance for democracy: in the first place, they serve to formulate clearly the policies that are presented to the electorate; secondly, they arouse the interest of the electorate in these policies; and thirdly they ensure that the victorious policy is in fact binding on the ensuing government. This second process culminates in the theory of 'the mandate'.

It has been observed by political writers that the second process when complete has succeeded to some extent in undoing or reversing the first process. For though the life of the government continues to depend upon the will of the Commons, during its life the government now manages to enforce its will upon the Commons; and it manages to do so because it is in effect the organ of party leadership.

6. THE FEARS OF DEMOCRACY. The constant feature that runs through nineteenth-century thought, both conservative and

liberal, is the fear of democracy. For the most part this is of an entirely *a priori* kind. All arguments. for intance, about democracy as the cause of lower cultural standards (Carlyle, Lecky, Henry Adams) are necessarily of this kind since then, as now, there was not even a rudimentary sociology of art. Some of the arguments, however, are more empirical in character. In the middle of the century the great soucebook for those who were rationally frightened of democratic excesses was Alexis de Tocqueville's *De la démocratie en l'Amérique* (1835). Tocqueville has, however, been much misunderstood. He was not an enemy of democracy: he was, rather, so convinced of its coming victory that he passed over its advantages and concentrated on its defects and dangers. Towards the end of the century and at the beginning of the twentieth century, most anxiety about democracy finds fresh sustenance in the findings of the new science of psychology. Originally these findings were the preserve of those who were openly and actively hostile to democracy, but gradually they were taken up by a considerable body of thinkers who were basically favourable to democracy and wanted to find a way of reconciling their beliefs with the new science. These range from optimistic thinkers like Graham Wallas to more pessimistic thinkers like Walter Lippmann.

7. DEMOCRACY AND ECONOMICS. To eighteenth- and early nineteenth-century democrats the natural corollary of their political beliefs seemed to be the economic doctrines of *laissez-faire*. A few radical voices were raised in protest against this prevailing orthodoxy, but to no great effect. However, from the middle of the nineteenth century onwards the traditional view of the correct economic implications of democratic belief was increasingly called in doubt. It became apparent that democracy implied *laissez-faire* only on certain further assumptions, largely of a psychological and economic character, that were not themselves justified. The main psycological assumption was a thoroughgoing egoism inherited from eighteenth-century mechanistic theory, but which found little support in empirical psychology. The most significant economic assumption was that the theoretical requirements of perfect competition were in fact satisfied under ordinary conditions; increasingly did it become

apparent to orthodox economists that in practice monopolistic
and semi-monopolistic conditions are inevitable.[10]

Contemporary discussion of democracy may be brought under four rough headings: the *meaning* of democracy, the *conditions* of democracy, the *justification* of democracy, and the
relation of democracy to other political concepts and principles.

1. The problem of the meaning of democracy arises as soon as
one considers with any degree of literalness the word itself:
demo-cracy, the 'rule of the people'. For contrast this with
other similar words, such as *pluto-cracy*, 'rule of the rich', and
theo-cracy, the 'rule of the priests'.[11] Immediately two questions
assert themselves. In the first place, how can the people rule in
the way in which the rich or the priests clearly can? For surely
there are too many of them for it to be a practical possibility.
And secondly, if the people rule, who is there left to be
ruled? (It is to be observed that in the classical world neither
of these two questions arose with the force that they do for us.
For in the first place, the City State was generally small enough
to permit the people to participate directly in government.
Secondly, to most classical thinkers the word 'demos' meant
the people in the sense of 'the common people' or 'the ordinary
man', or, more simply, 'the poor', not in the modern sense of
'the people as a whole', or 'every member of society': in consequence if the demos ruled, this left the rich and the noble to be
ruled over.)

Two traditions of democratic thought can be identified by the
way in which they treat this problem. One tradition, stemming
ultimately from Rousseau, insists on taking this problem very
literally and proposing to it a radical and peculiar solution. To
begin with, all the members of society are said to possess two
wills or selves: a 'true' or 'real' self, and an 'arbitrary' or
'fitful' self. All the true selves in any community are harmonious in their demands, whereas it is a mark of the arbitrary
selves that they are discordant. In terms of this para-psycholo-
gical assumption the two questions outlined above – or the 'paradox of self-government', as a thinker of this school, Bernard

Bosanquet called it – are readily solved. For to the first question, how can the people rule, being so many and so diverse?, the reply comes that it is their better selves that rule, and these selves, though naturally diverse, are necessarily harmonious. Secondly, to the question, who remains to be ruled if everyone rules?, the answer is given that though in a democracy the ruled are certainly different from the rulers as much as they are in a plutocracy or in a theocracy, they are however different, not in being different people, but in being different parts of the same people – that is, the ruled are the arbitrary or fitful selves of those whose real or true selves are the rulers.[12]

This tradition of thought, for all its metaphysical neatness, would appear to raise as many problems as it solves; and these further problems to be debarred of solution. For no empirical method is suggested whereby we can recognize or pick out the dictates of the true or real selves as opposed to those of the arbitrary selves. Indeed, when, as usually happens in this tradition of thought, the true self is further identified with the moral self, it is clear that no such method could be provided without falling into the errors of ethical Naturalism. From all this one might well assume that this 'idealist' tradition of democratic thought would lead to a total and barren scepticism about democratic practice. In fact the result has been rather different. Idealist thinkers have been led to support the notion of a supreme legislator or leader who would be able to penetrate the surface of conflicting individual desires and intuit the underlying rational and harmonious will of the community. Such a conception has been called 'totalitarian democracy'.[13] If in Anglo-American political thought, little or no attention has ever been paid by 'idealist' thinkers to this very difficult problem of the practical interpretation of their theory, such self-denial, though saying something for their political wisdom, scarcely redounds to their intellectual credit.

A different answer to this problem is provided by a school of thought, more empiricist in outlook, which seeks to remove the so-called paradox at an earlier stage. On this view, though in a democracy the people rule, they do not rule in the sense in which the rich might rule in a plutocracy or the priests in a theocracy; that is to say, they do not rule in the sense of holding in their own hands and wielding directly the supreme legislative and executive powers. They rule in a modified sense in that they exercise some control over the use of these powers. And in this sense of ruling, the argument continues, there can be no difficulty in seeing how the people, many of them though there may be, can rule. Equally, on this view, there is no difficulty in seeing how the people can at once rule and be ruled. For the supreme legislative and executive powers, like any other external force or instrument, can be controlled *by* a group of people and yet also exercised *over* that group. The empiricist solution differs from the idealist solution above in that the paradox that is supposed to arise from the fact that the rulers and the ruled are in a democracy identical, is disposed of, not by any dialectical legerdemain leading to a radical reinterpretation of political experience, but by an analysis which seeks to understand the concept of 'rule' or 'government' as it appears in the context of democratic thought, without in any way altering it.

However, it would be a mistake to assume that this empiricist view does not also give rise to further problems. For though it may answer the difficulties connected with the size or vastness of the ruling group in a democracy, it still leaves unsettled those which arise or are alleged to arise out of its diversities and disharmonies. If the people do not agree upon how the supreme legislative and executive powers of the community are to be used – as they most likely will not – how can they control the use of these powers? Such difficulties certainly exist. It is, however, error to regard these as metaphysical or logical, rather than practical, difficulties. For there is no absurdity or inconsistency or self-contradiction in supposing the people to exert control over policy even when the policy pursued is not to the taste of all. The only issue is whether the method employed for selecting policy by aggregating tastes is 'reasonable' or 'fair', and this issue is practical.

In Anglo-Saxon countries the usual method employed for ensuring popular control is that of representative institutions with a composition determined by specific electoral procedures, and these methods have over the years been found to satisfy the natural or intuitive demands of 'reasonableness' and 'fairness'. However, it needs to be emphasized that all these devices are no more than well-tried means of securing democratic control: none of them logically guarantees such control.

Though much of the criticism levelled at representative institutions is grossly exaggerated in that it assimilates the abuses of the system to its necessary concomitants, it does provide certain healthy reminders of how the system can go wrong. These may be brought under four headings:

(i) The society may be so sunk in apathy or swept away by hysteria that the majority vote is untypical of the considered ideas and desires of the majority of the society. To guard against apathy certain democratic countries have introduced compulsory voting (Australia, Belgium, Switzerland, etc.). In spite of the arguments that can be put forward in favour of this measure – most of which were raised in the debates in the Australian Parliament on its introduction in 1924 – it has generally been regarded as 'undemocratic' in itself. Against mass hysteria no plausible constitutional safeguard has yet been proposed.

(ii) The society may be entirely reasonable and balanced in its voting habits, and yet, through some technical aspect of the electoral procedure, it may be impossible to arrive at a decision that can properly be said to represent the wishes of the majority. The limiting case which arises for any electoral procedure is where each of the alternatives voted upon attracts an equal number of voters, for then no decision whatsoever is forthcoming. A more difficult case is where a decision is forthcoming, but this clearly does not tally with what ordinarily or intuitively would be thought to be the majority will. It can be demonstrated that for every known 'reasonable' method of voting if the alternatives are three or more there is a situation in which this is bound to happen.[14] The only absolutely foolproof system is where every elector votes in turn on every pair of alternatives – a scarcely practical method.[15] (Proportional representation, often at this stage recommended as a panacea, merely transfers these difficulties from the electoral stage to the legislative stage.)

(iii) The society may know its own mind, express it unequivocally through the electoral procedure, and then the majority so established may enforce its policy with a complete disregard for the desires, interests or rights of the minority. Fears of the 'tyranny of the majority' were a constant theme in the nineteenth century, the great age of democratic thought. In the twentieth century, the great age of democratic practice, these fears have not on the whole been realized – though, significantly, where they have been, the reality has been on a scale far exceeding the worst envisaged. It would seem that the problem here is sociological rather than political, in that social conditioning is more likely to be an effective remedy than a system of constitutional checks and balances.

(iv) The majority may know its own mind, express it through the electoral mechanism, and the majority so constituted so far from tyrannizing over the minority, may fail even to exert rule over it. For power can fall into the hands of a minority within the majority. Some thinkers have indeed claimed that any machinery of majority rule is bound to put effective control into the hands of a minority. But this would seem to be exaggeration. Since the end of the last century, increasing attention has, how-ever, been paid to the oligarchic tendencies implicit in demo-cratic machinery: in particular, those relating to party organiza-tion and programme construction.

Perhaps the most important single lesson to be learnt from these objections is that democracy cannot be self-guarantee-ing. It is exposed to risks, in the first place, from the mechanism that is devised to implement it, and secondly, from the other ele-ments in society. It has been called justifiably, a 'calculated risk'.[16]

2. The question of the conditions of democracy, i.e., what must exist for democracy to exist, is one of the great problems of the age. Unfortunately, a great deal of contemporary discussion of it is bedevilled by an essential ambiguity in the nature of the question. It is often unclear whether the question is *logical*, i.e., what conditions must be satisfied for us to say correctly that democracy exists, or *empirical*, i.e., what conditions must exist elsewhere in society for democracy to come into existence and to survive.[17] Such ambiguity is common in theoretical argu-ments, but in this context there are two additional factors to account for its persistence. One is the absence of any developed sociology of politics; and the other is the extreme prestige

attached to the word 'democracy', so that writers tend to take over any concomitant of democracy that they like and write about it as if it were part of democracy.

In contemporary discussions of the conditions of democracy, three issues have been singled out for particular attention:

(i) The connection between democracy and socialism. Those who assert that there is a real connection between the two may be divided into three groups:

First, there are the Marxists. These are sometimes taken to assert that democracy is incomplete without socialism. This, however, is a misunderstanding of their true position. For what they wish to do is not so much to extend the concept of democracy as to transpose it completely. Believing in what has been called the 'impotence of politics',[18] they are indifferent to constitutional and political organization, but at the same time want to secure the full prestige of this concept for their own preference in what they consider to be the truly important field – that of economic organization. It is significant that the use of the word 'democracy' as a word of praise in Marxist thought dates from the time when it became a universally honorific word.

Secondly, there are the democratic socialists. Of these the Guild Socialists used to argue that a society could not truly be called 'democratic' unless all the institutions in it were themselves democratic. Amongst these institutions were to be numbered factories and other industrial plants, and the democratization of such institutions necessarily involves workers' control, i.e., socialism.[19] Nowadays, most socialists would prefer to use less *a priori* arguments. Some would use a pragmatic argument, namely that political democracy cannot be truly safe without economic reorganization: and again others would prefer a moral argument to the effect that there is an inconsistency in applying the principle of equality in the field of politics and denying it in the field of economics.

Thirdly, there are the conservatives who argue that democracy is in its nature incompatible with socialism. There are a number of arguments raised in current discussion to this effect: they are differentiated according to the feature of democracy that they hold to be the ground of this incompatibility. Some have held this to be competition, others tolerance, others the existence of property. A recent argument that has attracted attention is that which maintains that democracy requires freedom, freedom requires the Rule of Law, and socialism in its advocacy of bureaucratic planning has to dispense with the Rule of Law.[20] Against this it has been urged in the first place, that the Rule of Law guarantees security, not freedom; and secondly, that even if economic planning does contract freedom in some directions, it extends it in others and the overall effect may well be an increase rather than a diminution.[21]

(ii) The connection between democracy and the belief in democracy. Since John Stuart Mill who claimed (ironically enough) that democracy was not suitable for 'Malays and Bedouins', it has been generally conceded by even the most fervent democrats that there are some conditions that a population must satisfy for it to be fit for democracy. However, despite the practical urgency of this problem with the break-up of the old colonial empires, our knowledge of what these conditions are has not increased. On one condition – which to some appears to have a certain intuitive obviousness – controversy has been bitter: viz., the belief in, or acceptance of, democracy. Now if this condition is taken as applying to society as a whole it is obviously true, perhaps logically so. But it does not follow from this that it is therefore true of every single member of a society. Society to be democratic must believe in democracy; but how many members it can successfully contain who do not themselves believe in democracy, is a question incapable of any *a priori* answer. It depends on the restraints that these dissidents are prepared to put upon their own behaviour, on the moral or spiritual authority that they wield over others, and on the extent to which their behaviour can be neutralized by other factors in society (free speech, the press, education, etc.).

(iii) The connection between democracy and constitutionalism. It would be common ground to nearly all supporters of democracy that there are certain laws or regulations that ought not to be passed even if the greater part or indeed the whole of the people favour them. To some it has seemed desirable to inscribe these 'moral limitations' of democracy in a charter or constitution. Some English thinkers have gloried in the fact that liberties enjoyed in Great Britain are to be found not in any constitution but in the accumulated precedents of common law.[22] It would seem, however, that though this may well be something to be grateful for, it is not a matter for pride, and it is perfectly natural that other, and in particular younger, democracies should prefer to express their ideals in a more systematic if necessarily more 'artificial' fashion.

However, the issue somewhat changes when the constitution is regarded not merely as a systematic statement of the liberties recognized in society but as a method of guaranteeing them. In such cases the constitution is accompanied by some mechanism for enforcing provisions like that of judicial review. To certain thinkers this has seemed the obvious requirement of democracy; by others it has been regarded as inequitable, incompetent, and unnecessary. It is inequitable because it tries to limit the power of the living majority by means of the 'the dead hand' of the past: it is incompetent because the only cases where it is likely to arise are just those where the constitution itself will require 'interpretation'; and it is unnecessary because a society that is likely to accept the findings of such a mechanism is unlikely seriously to offend against the spirit of its constitution. These strictures are sometimes supported by a historical examination of the record of actual mechanisms, e.g., the history of 'judicial review' in the U.S. as an instrument of democracy.[23]

3. There are in circulation in Anglo-Saxon thought a number of arguments, all purporting to justify democracy. These arguments vary greatly in acceptability according to the number and validity of the principles they invoke, the truth of the factual assumptions they make use of, and the relevance of the kind of democracy for which they argue to the kind that we experience.

(i) To exercise rule or to enjoy any form of political authority is a kind of moral education. On egalitarian grounds the opportunity for such self-improvement should be extended to as many as possible. In democracy it is extended to all: therefore democracy is the best of all forms of government. This argument, which is originally to be found in Aristotle (*Pol.* III. 1277b), may have had some application within the confines of the Polis, but applied to the conditions of the modern world it seems hopelessly unrealistic. Significantly enough, it is the characteristic argument of a kind of liberalism which is or was peculiarly associated with a classical education.

(ii) The second argument is that true opinion on political and moral matters is the privilege of the common man. Accordingly, power in a community should reside with him: and this it does only in a democracy. Hence the superiority of democracy. As we have seen, this argument is central to the Greek conception of democracy. In modern thought it has received reinforcement from a certain sentimental theory of the goodness of human nature uncorrupted by wealth, luxury and education. In contrast to this, democracy has come in for much criticism based on the so-called discovery of man's 'irrationality' by modern psychology. Much of this criticism is confused, and, if it proves anything, proves not so much the weakness of democracy as the weakness of this particular argument for it.

(iii) A more materialistic version of the preceding argument makes the ordinary man the best judge not of what is right for the community but of his own interests. In consequence, if the people are allowed to control the government, then the interests of the people will be dominant. Democracy is identified with popular control, and therefore vindicated. This argument is the argument of the Utilitarians, supported in their case by a thoroughgoing psychological egoism. It also has been subjected to a great deal of empirical criticism. Recent sociology has, for instance, cast doubt on the classical notions of class by bringing out what has been called (perhaps misleadingly) the 'subjective' element in class determination. Nevertheless the argument has considerable weight.

(iv) A further retreat from the positions maintained in the two previous arguments leads to the completely sceptical argument for democracy. According to this argument, it is impossible for anyone to discover what is the right course of action for the community, or where the true interests of its inhabitants reside. From this it follows that everyone in the community should be allowed to do what he wants to do as far as is socially possible. The only society in which this can happen is the one in which everyone has some control in the government: therefore democracy is favoured. As a variant of this argument, it may be maintained that even if one can discover what is ideally the right course of action to pursue, it would be wrong to insist on it unless everyone in the community recognized its rightness. Accordingly in practice one must adopt a sceptical attitude towards government and allow people to have the laws, institutions, etc., that they want: hence democracy.

It seems to be certainly the case that scepticism does involve democracy – even if the link is not as rigorous or as formal as some would believe. It does not follow from this, though – as certain critics of democracy would have us believe – that democracy involves scepticism.

(v) At the opposite end of the scale it is maintained that everyone has a natural right to control government and that this right is recognized only in democracy: therefore democracy is the best form of government. This argument has been subjected to two lines of criticism, both of which are misguided. The first is that the conception of 'a natural right' is metaphysical. Now natural rights are capable of, and often receive, a metaphysical interpretation, but this is not necessary. To say that something is a natural right may merely be a way of saying that it is an ultimate value. Secondly, it has been urged that it is absurd to allow that everyone has a natural right to exercise control over government when in fact not everyone can do so. But this argument assumes that the right in question is, in the terminology of jurisprudence, 'a right proper' (i.e., correlative to duty) whereas it seems more natural to assume that it is a liberty or privilege.[24]

(vi) Finally, it may be maintained that it is irrelevant whether democracy does in fact maximize welfare, safeguard rights, accord with natural law, etc., for the fact is that under modern conditions it is the only working possibility. No member of an emancipated industrial society will put up with political tutelage. He insists on having a fair chance of influencing the government in accordance with his own desires and ideas; and by a 'fair' chance he means a chance 'as good as the next man's'. This argument was succinctly summarized in the nineteenth century by the conservative James Fitz-James Stephen who said that in democracy we count heads to avoid breaking them; and it remains today one of the best arguments in favour of democracy on account of its extreme economy.

4. The relation of the concept of democracy to other notions such as equality, liberty, etc., falls outside the scope of this article.

REFERENCES

1. J. A. O. Larsen, 'Judgment of Antiquity on Democracy', *Classical Philology*, 49 (1954), 1–4.
2. A. Debrunner, *Festschrift für E. Tièche* (Bern, 1947), 11–24; Victor Ehrenberg, 'Origins of Democracy', *Historia* (1950), 515–48; J. A. O. Larsen, 'Cleisthenes and the Development of the Theory of Democracy at Athens', *Essays in Political Theory Presented to George H. Sabine* (Ithaca, 1948), 1–16.
3. Gregory Vlastos, "Isonomia", *American Journal of Philology*, 74 (1953), 337–66.
4. J. A. O. Larsen, *Representative Government in Greek and Roman History* (Berkeley-Los Angeles, 1955).
5. A. S. P. Woodhouse, *Puritanism and Liberty* (London, 1948).
6. Elisha P. Douglass, *Rebels and Democrats* (Chapel Hill, 1955).
7. Elie Halévy, *The Growth of Philosophical Radicalism* (London, 1928).
8. Sir Ivor Jennings, *Cabinet Government* (Cambridge, England, 1937).
9. M. Ostrogorsky, *Democracy and the Organization of Political Parties* (London, 1902).
10. J. M. Keynes, *The End of Laissez-Faire* (London, 1927).
11. G. A. Paul, "Democracy", *Chambers Encyclopaedia*, 4 (1944), 430–1.
12. Bernard Bosanquet, *The Philosophical Theory of the State* (London, 1899).
13. J. L. Talmon, *The Origins of Totalitarian Democracy* (London, 1952).
14. E. J. Nanson, "Methods of Election", *Transactions and Proceedings of the Royal Society of Victoria*, 19 (1883), 197–240; Kenneth Arrow, *Social Choices and Individual Values* (New York, 1951).
15. Robert A. Dahl, *A Preface to Democratic Theory* (Chicago, 1956).
16. Robert A. Dahl and Charles Lindblom, *Politics, Economics and Welfare* (New York, 1953).
17. Joseph A. Schumpeter, *Capitalism, Socialism and Democracy* (New York, 1947).
18. Karl R. Popper, *The Open Society and Its Enemies* (London, 1945).
19. G. D. H. Cole, *Guild Socialism Re-Stated* (London, 1920).
20. F. A. von Hayek, *The Road to Serfdom* (London, 1944).
21. Hans Kelsen, 'Democracy and Socialism', *Conference on Jurisprudence and Politics* (Chicago, 1954), 63–87.
22. A. V. Dicey, *Introduction to the Study of the Law of the Constitution* (London, 1885).

23. Henry S. Commager, *Majority Rule and Minority Rights* (New York–London, 1943).
24. Richard Wollheim and Isaiah Berlin, 'Equality', *Proceedings of the Aristotelian Society*, 30 (1956), 281–326.

Totalitarianism

ROBERT ORR

Robert Orr was born in New Zealand in 1927. Since 1963 he has been a senior lecturer in government at the London School of Economics.

His publications include: *Reason and Authority*, 1967, as well as many articles in academic journals.

Reflections on Totalitarianism

Robert Orr

The twentieth century includes among its dubious distinctions that of having added 'totalitarianism' to the political vocabulary of Europe – and to that of the rest of the world which in this, as in other respects, has followed Europe. The history of the word as a political idea has yet to be thoroughly written, but enough is known of its career in the mouths of the politically interested to enable some points of interest to be noted.[1]

It appears to have seen first limelight around 1925 in the speeches of Mussolini, prompted and informed by Gentile. As used then, and in those circumstances, *uno stato totalitario* signalled an approved state of affairs – national unity, the abolition of opposition parties, the end of sectional-interest domination. 'After years of divisive politics, we now have a government of national union', declared Mussolini, in phrases distinguishable only in their rough-and-readiness from those with which de Gaulle was later to announce the end of the Fourth Republic of France. General Franco used the term in Mussolini-copybook fashion, but only in the early, inexperienced years of his government, when verbal borrowings from a friendly source were especially welcome.[2]

In the English tongue, "totalitarianism" was used first in the *Quarterly Review* and *The Times* in the late 1920s, by writers concerned only to translate a foreign word, themselves contributing neither approval nor disapproval. But later, following the Nazi victory in Germany, the alleged assimilation of the Italian and German dictatorships to each other and the worsening of Anglo-German relations, the term came to be applied intermittently to all the Continental dictatorships. Further, it came to signify, in the English language at least, a political state of affairs which was entirely disapproved. There is considerable uncertainty about when the Soviet Union came to be bracketed with the other candidates for the term, but there was at least some disposition to do so before the Second World War,[3] a disposition which was muffled during the war period, but which revived with the onset of the cold war. Since the cold war, the term has invaded political writing at all levels, and has lent itself adjectivally to all manner of disapproved things. As well as totalitarian governments, regimes, systems, we have totalitarian ideas, policies, cultures, movements, parties, processes. The only regular feature of its usage appears to be a uniformly high level of expressed condemnation, mitigated not one iota by a recent belief that the cold war has of late lost some of its stark simplicity, nor even by some creeping doubts as to whether the Soviet Union should be called a totalitarian state.[4] The term, as we now have it, is part of the general vocabulary with which we attempt to hurt our enemies, national and international.

This chronicle of usage illustrates two general features, neither of which is uncommon in the history of political ideas. One is that the word has not remained constant in its moral colouring. Like the word 'puritan' in the sixteenth century, it started as a term of approval, then moved to the 'con' side of the board on which moral sentiments are registered, where it has thus far stayed. Indeed, it seems likely to become stuck there, a near-useless synonym for 'bad', if the efforts of political scientists to salvage an academic meaning for it fail.

The other feature is that the term has 'ramified' in its range of application.[5] From its roots of self-reference in Italian politics it has branched out to include the Third Reich, the Soviet Union, present-day Cuba, and, more recently, the United States.[6] As it has acquired new meanings it has modified, or lost, old ones. One writer, at least, always refused to extend the term to Mussolini's Italy, and, in her latest edition, demurs at its application to the Soviet Union.[7] In its short life in politics, then, the term has gone its self-willed way, accommodating new arrivals while dropping old ones, using precedents as it deems fit, but held by them only on the lightest of reins.

We turn now to the attempt to make a separate career altogether for it, in the world of theoretical understanding. One does not, of course, have to theorize about totalitarianism in order to write about it. Hannah Arendt's large and much-read book shows that there is interest enough in a work which moralizes in well-informed fashion about the miseries of our age – and assigns origins to them. It is equally beyond doubt that theoretical thinking began before serious written work appeared. As early as 1939 we see in significant print the belief – which was to motivate all later theorizing – that totalitarianism was a 'novel form of government' which would disclose to inspection certain features essential and peculiar to itself. In a lecture given in November of that year, Carlton Hayes called 'dictatorial totalitarianism' a revolt against Western civilization, traceable to the decline of organized religion, and to the emergence of national leaders who come from 'the masses rather than the classes'. This, so far, was the familiar enough formula of assigning causal antecedents to something disagreeable. But Hayes went further and elaborated the 'specific novelties' of totalitarian government, in a model which differs from later, more celebrated ones only in its brevity. They were:

(1) It is total, in the sense that it monopolizes all powers within the society.
(2) It commands and rests upon mass support.
(3) It is maintained by new, and uniquely effective techniques of education and propaganda.
(4) It exalts might and force.

This quadripartite analysis is an attempt, not to moralize about totalitarianism, nor to find its blameworthy origins, but to state the meaning of the concept in terms of its intrinsic components.[8] The other contributors to this symposium were concerned largely with what was going on in Germany and Italy. Hayes alone essayed a paper with theoretical aspirations.

The first post-war landmark in the story of theorizing was a meeting at Boston in March 1953 of the American Academy of Arts and Sciences. The miscellany who attended – and they included such diversities as George F. Kennan and Erik H. Erikson – shared little more than the conviction that totalitarianism had 'burst upon mankind more or less unexpected and unannounced', and that it was 'such an extraordinary and all-pervading phenomenon of our time that the best scholarly and scientific efforts should be marshalled, and the necessary funds provided . . . ' There were some present, however, notably Carl Friedrich, who addressed themselves to this question: we already have a battery of descriptive terms which we apply to highly centralized regimes – despotism, tyranny, dictatorship, autocracy. We know roughly where we are with these regime terms, whose meaning causes little difficulty, save at the margins. But totalitarianism? All we know for certain is that it is a hard-core political term, i.e. not part of the general vocabulary of ethics, that it is employed to designate sovereign states, and that it is used on the hustings to register unqualified disapproval. Can we find a 'scientific' employment for it? Is it possible, by removing, or at least mitigating the disapproval, to recreate it as a 'conceptual tool' which will tell us about the actual operations of a type of government which the world has hitherto not known? Can it, in short, be given the status of words like 'federal' or 'monarchical', which lend themselves to intellectual as well as to political usage?

Friedrich, who edited the published volume of papers which came out of the conference, thought that it could, and gave his first version of what was to become the staple analysis of the term in schools of political science.[9] The fuller version, which appeared three years later in the book written jointly with Zbigniew Brzezinski, set out to give 'a general descriptive theory of a novel form of government'.[10] The point of the book is not to explain, as did Hannah Arendt, how totalitarianism came to be, but to 'delineate the model'. The model they put forward is well-known: the concept of totalitarianism is a cluster, or syndrome, made up of six 'common features'.

(1) An elaborate ideology, i.e. an officially prescribed doctrine with something to say about all practical sides of life, including the proper way to anticipate the final state of the human race.
(2) A single mass party, led by a dictator, hierarchically organized, which permits no rivals. It is monolithic, i.e. it is in one piece, and there are no other pieces.
(3) Terroristic police control, which not only supports but supervises the party.
(4) Monopoly control of communications.

(5) A near-complete control of the armed forces.

(6) A centralized bureaucratic control of the economy. There is no 'pluralism', no permission of secondary associations to stand between the citizen and the state juggernaut.

The authors admit that the list might not be complete, and reserve the right to add other items to the syndrome should these convincingly show themselves.[11] In later editions, in fact, the formula is modified, and in Friedrich's latest version there is an attempt to telescope the syndrome into three, plus one with three variants. The 'generally accepted set of facts', we are now told, comprises:

(1) A totalist ideology.

(2) A single party committed to this ideology and usually led by one man, the dictator.

(3) A fully developed secret police.

(4) Three kinds of monopoly control:

    (a) mass communications

    (b) operational weapons

    (c) all organizations of a centrally planned economy.[12]

While conceding that the urge for simplicity might reduce the six to three ('a totalist ideology, a party reinforced by a secret police, and monopoly control of the three major forms of interpersonal confrontation in an industrial mass society'), Friedrich has stuck, in the face of widespread criticism, to his original conception of a properly shaped theory of totalitarianism. This conception is indicated in a repeated use of three terms with which he indicates the formal pretensions of the scheme. He calls it:

(1) A general morphological and operational theory.

(2) A delineation of the model.

(3) A set of 'principles of usage'.[13]

These phrases, and the actual course of the argument, display a certain conception of what it is to explain, if not all general political terms, at least this one, and I wish now to draw attention to four features of 'principles of usage', as Friedrich understands them – if you like, 'principles of principles of usage':

1. Principles of usage, understood in this way, recognize and retain the internal diversity of the concept, i.e. in theorizing about it you do not attempt to reduce it to one simple essential

idea. 'Totalitarianism' is thus understood to be a concept more like that of 'federalism' than that of 'monarchy' in that it has multiple components, and this multiplicity is preserved in the model. To abolish it would be to lose touch with usage, as Friedrich warns, when critizicing a recent paper of Brzezinski, from whom in recent years he has come to differ on the question of how it is proper to theorize about the matter. A theory which attempts to indicate the 'essence' of totalitarianism will not keep pace with a 'maturing concept' is the burden of Friedrich's criticism of the new-style Brzezinski.[14]

Further, although the diverse elements of the concept are 'mutually intertwined', and thereby support each other in building up the whole concept, their mutual connection is not necessary, nor is the list exhaustive; other features may be added. The concept is, in fact, a shopping list. Tick off the six items, and you have the concept in its thus far completed state. Whether any particular regime qualifies is a question of more and less, since 'totalitarian dictatorship, like other political phenomena, is a relative, not an absolute, term'.

2. Not only is the concept made up of mutually-assisting components, but the concept as a whole enjoys good relations with its conceptual neighbours and kinsfolk. Totalitarianism, understood in this way, does not exclude autocracy, dictatorship, tyranny.[15] Since any actual regime might be both totalitarian and autocratic, 'principles of usage' demand a model which is non-exclusive of such sister-terms.

3. Even if the concept, drawn in this way, will not distinguish itself absolutely from other concepts, it will serve to distinguish between actual governments. And governments, in the end, are what Friedrich is concerned to distinguish. In 1953, it is true, he was disposed to treat 'totalitarianism' as a term describing 'more than a form of government', i.e. a whole society, but he has apparently come to see its proper application as restricted to governments and regimes.[16] The six-point scale is designed to discriminate between the USSR of *Darkness at Noon* and the France or Britain of the mid-twentieth century. The very looseness, lack of generality or of abstract ambitions of the concept, delineated in this way, enable it to be used as a sorter-out of actual regimes, and is meant to do so.

4. The concept contains built into its formulation the moral sentiments of its ordinary usage. 'Terror', 'police-state', terms unmistakably conveying disapproval, are elemental to the meaning. What you feel about it is part of what it is. Hannah Arendt's book may be called an essay on the themes of terror and corruption, while Leonard Schapiro's recent analysis designates the exemplars of totalitarian leadership as 'sordid psychopaths and mountebanks'.[17]

Principles of usage, then, reflect the fact that political language is unsystematic, wayward, flexible, open to revision, hospitable to neighbourly invasion, and makes and breaks its rules as and when occasion seems to require. Theorizing in this manner can always demonstrate its relevance, its touch with 'reality', its responsibility to its paymasters.

It suffers one hazard: what is to become of it when the common usage of the term threatens to become so hopelessly ambiguous, so available to everybody that its serviceability as an indicator of actual societies is questionable? That something like this has happened recently there can be little doubt.[18]

Faced with this situation, the world-be theorist has three alternatives open to him:

1. To drop the enterprise altogether. This is the path taken, with steps of varying firmness, by Herbert Spiro, J. Kautsky, B. Barber and M. Curtis. Their given reasons range from allegations that the U.S.A. is, by the standards of the Friedrich model, crypto-totalitarian, to the general observation that the cold war, which gave the term its theoretical livelihood, is now irretrievably complicated.

2. To making running repairs to the theory. This is the way of Friedrich, who now seeks to accommodate 'mature totalitarianism', and the 'popular' versions of Cuba, Ghana and Yugoslavia.[19] It is also the way of Robert Tucker and Robert Burrowes, who, for diverse reasons, believe that the concept 'answers a genuine need of intellectual communication'.[20]

3. To strike out in a fresh theoretical direction altogether, i.e. to undertake not only a revised version of totalitarianism, but a revised (albeit ancient) way of theorizing. It is to theorize by attempting to define an essence rather than assemble a syndrome. This track, as is to be expected, is undertaken with the

greatest trepidation by political scientists – Brzezenski takes a step in this direction when he speaks openly of 'pointing to the essence' of totalitarianism as 'institutionalized revolutionary zeal', without, however, removing the other foot decisively from the old syndrome.[21]

One piece of writing has shown how a syndrome theory might, by perceptible steps, be reshaped towards an essentialist theory. Leonard Schapiro, in a seminar paper delivered at the London School of Economics, revealed two dissatisfactions with the Friedrich catalogue.

(1) It serves insufficiently to distinguish the regimes it purports to distinguish from others.

(2) It fails to define the concept exclusively; as it stands, the Friedrich syndrome is too miscellaneous.

Schapiro believes fault 1 stems from fault 2, and suggests that the answer is 'to subsume these general characteristics under more theoretical formulae'.[22] Schapiro, in short, believes (as did Friedrich) that there is something distinctive about the Nazi, Fascist and Soviet regimes taken as an ensemble – though he gives more weight to parallel features in other and older regimes than does Friedrich – and thinks the way to elucidate this is by defining the concept more tightly. He accordingly sets about stripping the Friedrich syndrome down to a more exclusive specification. First, the monopolistic monolithic party was in Stalin's hands only one agency among others exercising, and competing for, control.

Secondly, terror is not exclusive to these regimes, and the amount used will always be a matter of circumstance. Thirdly, none of these states has gained an ideological monopoly; to do so they would have to eliminate the church as a competitor. Fourthly, control over the economy is such a comparative and relative thing that it will hardly serve as an 'exclusive' (a key word of Schapiro's) characteristic.

Having stripped the concept of its superfluities, Schapiro offers a reformulation. All features which are distinctly totalitarian, he writes, are reducible to three entities:

(1) The existence of a 'mass society' (in Kornhauser's sense), as a 'precondition' for totalitarian government.

(2) The State's assertion of the right to 'total control' of society.

(3) The State's assertion of its right to 'control' all matters of morals and conscience.

From these three definitive principles Schapiro deduces the consequential components, which in fact take in most of Friedrich's particulars – centralization, intolerance of rival societies, etc. These are not built into the centrally-defined concept, but are seen as possible deductions from it. Whether you draw the deduction will depend upon how you read the society before you.

Schapiro has compressed the concept to three master-ideas. And looking at them, bearing in mind that the mass-society element is ranked only as a 'precondition', one is inclined to suggest that still further reduction is possible, that Schapiro is turning the whole concept around the master-notion of 'total control'. He would not be alone in doing so. Writers of an unmistakably philosophical disposition have typically defined a totalitarian society as one in which the relationship between rulers and subjects is comprehensive, and is totally regulated by the former.[23]

If we inspect the writings of those who use this master-idea, the source of its inspiration is not hard to detect. The idea of total control comes by way of analogy from the field of mechanics, a modern source of ideas for a modern way of government. Government, thought of in this way, is an institution or a person shaping utterly malleable materials to predetermined purposes. When you control a power unit you can regulate the fuel intake, the ignition timing, the r.p.m. and the transmission ratios to limits and tolerances which are sufficient enough. If anything gets out of hand, it is strictly an accident.

But 'total control' has a defect as well as an advantage at its source, namely, its apparent extravagance, when employed to describe what, even in these times, is still a human relationship. A whiff of scepticism – of the type put forward in much of the recent literature about the Soviet Union and Eastern Europe – is likely to blow it over. A man being frog-marched by four policemen may not unconvincingly be said to be in a situation resembling total control in the mechanical sense, and this only as long as we ignore his thoughts. But if political relationships are thought of as comprising persuasion, promise, threat, suggestion, negotiation, blandishment, bribery – do these lie easily within the master-idea of total control?

If an essentialist definition of a totalitarian state is called for, I would suggest as an alternative the idea of a *mobilized* society. This image has the advantage that its source lies in the experience of modern warfare, where totalitarianism in fact found its generation.[24] It is a less rigid notion than that of 'control', without being any less effective in permitting particularistic inferences to be drawn from it. From the militaristic essence of a mobilized society may be inferred:

(1) An elitist, monopolistic party – these are the officers in exclusive command of:
(2) A mass society, i.e. the other ranks.
(3) Despite this distinction, party and masses are reduced to a relationship of mutual equality by the common over-riding commission or purpose to which they are committed.
(4) This purpose derives from the presence of 'enemies', external and internal, against whom 'war' is ready to be conducted. The enemies may be other states, revisionists, poverty, even an adverse balance of payments.
(5) An ideology will be necessary to identify and condemn these enemies – and to indicate and praise one's allies.
(6) A centrally directed economy, which is a standard concomitant of modern warfare.

Other inferences could no doubt be drawn. The components are not assembled as a 'syndrome', but are drawn from a single elementary idea.

The concept, defined in this way, contrasts in its formal properties with those of the Friedrich syndrome. It is:

(1) Simple, not multiple. Attention is drawn to a single analogy; a totalitarian society is said not to be an army, but understood as like an army at the ready. And, as with all analogies, it can be shaped as a paradox. Just as Hobbes spoke of the state as an 'artificial man' – an intolerable antimony in the old terms of Greek philosophy – so we are here transposing the items of the hitherto watertight dualism between a mobilized army and a civil society.
(2) Exclusive of others, and shows in the inferences where it differs from them. For example, from an authoritarian

state; Schapiro expresses doubt about the continued life of this term on the ground that *auctoritas* is a feature of any state. But 'authoritarianism', with its unmistakable ecclesiastical and Roman law origins, not only has the validity of continued usage, but can be defined in a way which separates it sharply from a totalitarian society. An authoritarian state may be said to be one where the primary and ultimate instrument of government is the assertion of its own legitimacy. It comes from an age, the Reformation, or Tudor England, when the church or the government was constantly having to answer, and if possible extinguish, the claims of rival contenders to office, holy or less-than-holy. Its paradigm in usage is probably the doctrine of papal infallibility. The morality appropriate to authoritarian states or churches, and totalitarian societies is clearly differentiated; one demands loyalty, the other solidarity

(3) It cannot be guaranteed to distinguish absolutely between one actual society and another. What it defines is something universal; you must expect to find it in all examples of the class specified, in this case in all modern societies. Herbert Marcuse and Charles Reich have had little difficulty in drawing the U.S.A. as a society in a state of mobilization, albeit a not very efficient one.

The classical philosophers made a practice of defining universals, or general ideas, by finding them in what had hitherto been thought of as unlikely places. For Plato, the elementary *polis* was located in the small economic association; for Aristotle, it lay in the family.

(4) It does not carry any necessary moral sentiment with it. When Plato defined a just society as one which realizes the division of labour, he recommended that the blueprint be copied; but the recommendation is not part of the outline. Hobbes's definition of Leviathan as artificial man is likewise no more than the centre-piece of a system of ideas, itself recommending or condemning nothing. And a 'mobilized society', or a 'totally controlled' one, is available for either praise, blame, or neither.

To sum up: the catalogue, or syndrome way of theorizing, is an attempt to reach heaven without letting your feet off the ground. Its advantage may be seen as a certain specificity which, given suitable company, can be used to distinguish between actual particulars before you. It is vulnerable to attack both from above and below – not rigorous enough for heaven, not detailed enough for earth.

To reach for an essential definition, whether of 'totalitarianism', 'democracy', 'liberty', or any general idea, is an undertaking of *hubris*, safe only for those whom the gods – not publishing houses – have commissioned. Otherwise, it will likewise be execrated both from above and below. Philosophers, as has long been recognized, are men fit neither for heaven nor earth. The gods will not overlook the presumptuous snatching of their exclusive right to make ultimate distinctions, any more than men will forgive the deprivation of their ability to use them.

REFERENCES

1. See L. Schapiro, *Totalitarianism* (London, 1972), ch. 1.
2. G. Hills, *Franco: The Man and His Nation* (London, 1967), p. 380.
3. See *Proceedings of the American Philosophical Society*, 1940. Symposium on 'The Totalitarian State', in particular the paper by Carlton J. H. Hayes.
4. See B. Barber in *Totalitarianism in Perspective* (London, 1969), p. 41.
5. See C. S. Lewis, *Studies in Words* (Cambridge, 1960), Introduction.
6. H. Marcuse, *One Dimensional Man* (London, 1964), and C. Reich, *The Greening of America* (London, 1971).
7. H. Arendt, *The Origins of Totalitarianism*, first published in 1951, see 1958 edition p. 308, and 1966 edition. See also M. Curtis in *Totalitarianism in Perspective*, p. 115.
8. Carlton J. H. Hayes, 'The Novelty of Totalitarianism in the History of Western Civilisation' in *Proceedings of the American Philosophical Society*, 1940.
9. C. J. Friedrich, 'The Unique Character of Totalitarian Society' in *Totalitarianism*, ed. Friedrich (Harvard, 1954).
10. C. J. Friedrich and Z. Brzezinski, *Totalitarian Dictatorship and Autocracy* (Harvard, 1956), Preface and Introduction. For a detailed record of the modifications undergone by this formula, see Schapiro, op. cit., ch. 2.
11. Ibid., p. 10.
12. *Totalitarianism in Perspective*, p. 126.

13. *Totalitarian Dictatorship and Autocracy*, Preface and Introduction.
14. *Totalitarianism in Perspective*, p. 127. He also rebukes Brzezinski for ceasing to find the Soviet Union totalitarian. See also Brzezinski, *Ideology and Power in Soviet Politics* (New York, 1967), ch. 1.
15. Ibid., p. 126.
16. Compare *Totalitarianism*, p. 4, with *Totalitarianism in Perspective*, p. 26. Schapiro (op cit., p. 20) makes a distinction between 'contours of a polity' and mere 'instruments of rule', and, in suggesting that totalitarianism is more tellingly detected in the former, indicates that for him the term denotes a whole society, not just a regime.
17. Op. cit., p. 21.
18. See Herbert Spiro's 'Totalitarianism' in *New Encyclopedia of Social Sciences*, 1968; the contributions by Michael Curtis and Benjamin Barber to *Totalitarianism in Perspective;* Z. Brzezinski, 'The Soviet Political System: Transformation or Degeneration?' in *Problems of Communism*, January–February 1966, p. 1ff.; R. Burrowes, 'Totalitarianism – The Revised Standard Version' in *World Politics*, January 1969; J. Kautsky, *Political Change in Underdeveloped Countries, Nationalism and Communism* (New York, 1962), p. 90; P. J. O'Brien, 'On the Adequacy of the Concept of Totalitarianism' in *Studies in Comparative Communism*, January 1970.
19. See 1967 edition, of which Friedrich was sole reviser, of *Totalitarian Dictatorship and Autocracy*, p. 53, and 'The Evolving Theory and Practice of Totalitarian Regimes' in *Totalitarianism in Perspective*.
20. Burrowes, op. cit., p. 294; R. C. Tucker, 'Towards a Comparative Politics of Movement Regimes' in *American Political Science Review*, June 1961, p. 283.
21. See 'Totalitarianism and Rationality' in *American Political Science Review*, September 1956, and *Ideology and Power in Soviet Politics*, ch. 1.
22. L. B. Schapiro, *Some Reflections on Totalitarianism*, cyclostyled seminar paper, p. 5.
23. See A. J. M. Milne, *Freedom and Rights* (London, 1968), p. 308. 'A totalitarian government is an unlimited government. Its scope extends to everything. Economic life, the arts, sciences, sport and entertainment, religion, even family life and personal relations, are subject to control and direction. Unlike a despotic government, a totalitarian government is never silent. It pronounces upon everything. There is no escape from the all-embracing grasp of government.' S. Andreski in *A Dictionary of the Social Sciences*, ed. L. Kolb and J. Gould (London, 1964), pp. 719–20 writes 'Totalitarianism is the extension of permanent governmental control over the totality of social life'. Herbert Spiro, in the article cited, suggests that the idea of total control is central to the whole Friedrich catalogue.
24. When the term 'totalitär' was first used in Germany, in 1930, by Ernst Juenger, it meant simply military mobilization. See Schapiro, op. cit., p. 13.

Nationalism

HANS KOHN

Hans Kohn was born in 1891 in Prague, Czechoslovakia. He emigrated to the United States in 1933. He was Professor of History at City College, New York from 1949 and a member of the Foreign Policy Research Institute at the University of Pennsylvania.

His publications include: *Force or Reason: Issues of the Twentieth Century*, 1937; *Revolutions and Dictatorships: Essays in Contemporary History*, 1939; *The Idea of Nationalism: A Study in Its Origins and Background*, 1944; *Prophets and Peoples: Studies in Nineteenth Century Nationalism*, 1946; *The Twentieth Century: A Mid-Way Account of the Western World*, 1949; *Pan-Slavism: Its History and Ideology*, 1953; *Nationalism: Its Meaning and History*, 1955; *Nationalism and Liberty: The Swiss Example*, 1956.

Nationalism

Hans Kohn

Nationalism is a political creed that underlies the cohesion of
modern societies and legitimizes their claim to authority. Nationalism centers the supreme loyalty of the overwhelming
majority of the people upon the nation-state, either existing or
desired. The nation-state is regarded not only as the ideal,
'natural', or 'normal' form of political organization but also
as the indispensable framework for all social, cultural, and
economic activities. Yet nationalism and the nation-state are
comparatively recent historical developments.

Unknown before the eighteenth century, when it originated
in northwestern Europe and northern America, nationalism
spread with ever-growing rapidity over all the earth, and since
the middle of the twentieth century it has become a universal
idée-force of contemporary history. It expresses itself in the
most varied and opposite ideologies – in democracy, fascism,
and communism – as well as in the search for an 'ideology', be
it African personality or Arab unity. The nineteenth century
in Europe has been rightly called the age of nationalism; the
twentieth century, in which history has shifted from a European
to a global basis, may become known as the age of pan-nation-
alism.

Although certain traits are common to all forms of nationalism, each form is conditioned by the social structure, the intellectual traditions and cultural history, and the geographic
location of the society in which nationalism asserts itself. Therefore, only a comparative historical study of the various forms
of nationalism can do justice to any one of them; and only an
interdisciplinary approach will be able to cover the many facets
of a highly complex phenomenon. No major collective research effort has yet been undertaken in this field, in spite of
its vital importance for an understanding of the contemporary
world.

The spread of nationalism on a global scale is a result of the

Europeanization and modernization of non-Western and pre-modern societies. As a phenomenon of modern European history, the rise of nationalism is closely linked with the origins of popular sovereignty; the theory of government by the active 'consent of the governed'; the growth of secularism; the lessening of the older religious, tribal, clannish, or feudal loyalties; and the spread of urbanization, industrialization, and improved communications.

Nationalism has from the beginning been a politically revolutionary movement; it has tried to transform or overthrow the 'legitimate' governments of the past whose claim to authority was based upon divine ordination or hereditary rights. It wished to establish totally new political entities: states coextensive with ethnic or linguistic frontiers. Lord Acton, in his famous essay 'Nationality' (1862), drew attention to the potentially dangerous implications of this identification of political organization with ethnic divisions. Within one hundred years (1815–1920), nationalism completely transformed the political map of central, central-eastern, and south-eastern Europe; and since 1947 it has fulfilled the same revolutionary function in remaking the political configuration of Asia and Africa.

The twentieth century has added another revolutionary dimension to nationalism. Nationalism has also become a socially revolutionary movement, demanding equal economic and educational opportunities for all members of the national group and the active promotion of the welfare of the socially underprivileged classes. Its aims have become the establishment of a classless, theoretically equalitarian national society. By the middle of the twentieth century, all 'young' nationalist movements had also become 'socialist' movements – the word 'socialism' covering as many different manifestations as the word 'nationalism' – whereas the 'young' nationalist movements of the middle of the nineteenth century had sharply distinguished between nationalism and socialism.

Nationalism, in the second half of the nineteenth century, was regarded as the political doctrine of the upper classes, of the rightists in the political spectrum of the age. It stood in sharp and repressive opposition to socialism, an international movement that included the industrial workers and landless peasants, who generally felt excluded from the national society, and expressed their aspirations. In the German empire that Bismarck created in 1871, the nationalists regarded the workers as *vaterlandslose Gesellen*, and Bismarck's anti-socialist legislation, 1878–1890, treated them as enemies of the nation. This Bismarckian attitude of Germany's ruling classes continued under the Weimar republic and was one of the main factors causing its overthrow. The situation in France, Italy, Spain, or Russia was not very different. There, too, the right-wing parties and the upper classes identified themselves with the nation and the national interest, and the lower classes felt excluded from both a real stake in the national economy and an active partnership in their determination of the policy of 'their' nation.

The first major nationalist revolution that put equal emphasis on the socialist revolutionary aspect was the Mexican revolution of 1910–1917. It set the pattern for the development of nationalism in many underdeveloped countries and for their fight against foreign political intervention and economic penetration and exploitation. Such an integration of nationalist and socialist revolutions was not, and could not be, attempted in the nineteenth century. The Polish aspirations for independence in the period of 1830 to 1848 were unsuccessful largely because the nationalist movement was upper-class; the peasantry had no interest in it and even turned against the landowners and urban intelligentsia. But even after World War I the nationalist revolutions of Kemal Atatürk in Turkey and of the Kuomintang under Chiang Kai-shek in China neglected the need for social transformations of their nations. As the upheavals in Turkey in1960/ 1961 and the defeat of Chiang Kai-shek in 1949 revealed, the economic and social positions of the present masses in both countries had remained backward; they continued to feel themselves victims of 'exploitation', but under the impact of nationalism they were ceasing to accept their age-old status passively. Only after World War II did socialism become an integral part of the nationalist revolution, as in Gamal Abdel Nasser's Egypt, in Ben Bella's Algeria, in Fidel Castro's Cuba, and in Sékou Touré's Guinea – to name only a few outstanding examples. This development resembles the transformation of the nineteenth-century capitalistic nation-state into the twentieth-century welfare state, except that in the underdeveloped countries truly radical social reforms were required. This task was made more difficult by the need of simultaneously building a cohesive national society, a need that, on the whole, had been fulfilled in the advanced countries by the time of World War I.

Nationalism, despite its relatively brief history, has undergone several transformations. It was an elite movement in the first century of its historic role; a 'bourgeois' movement in the age of the ascent of the middle classes; it has become, in its second century, a mass movement in which the people at large demand an ever-widening participation in the political, social, and cultural life of the nation.

What remains constant in nationalism through all its changes is the demand of the people for a government of the same ethnic complexion as the majority. Every people awakened to nationalism sees political self-determination as its goal. To be separate, distinct, and independent from other nations, and equal to them, is the fundamental claim of nationalists for their people. The 'individualism' and 'democratic equality' of the revolutions of the Enlightenment expressed themselves in these aspirations. In the nineteenth century these demands were transferred from the individual to the collective group. Only thus, said the nationalists, could the people become autonomous subjects, an end in themselves, instead of being a means for the policy of others. The Piedmontese jurist and Italian minister Pasquale Stanislao Mancini expressed this sentiment in his *Della nazionalità come fondamento del diritto delle genti* (1851), in a classical formulation: 'The nationalities which do not possess a government issuing from their innermost life (*governo uscito dalle proprie viscere*), and which are subject to laws imposed upon them from the outside . . . have become means for the purposes of others and, therefore, mere objects.'

CULTURAL SELF-DETERMINATION. Political self-determination is only one part of the demands inherent in all nationalism; an almost equal role is played by demands for cultural self-determination. In nationalities that are striving for the creation of a nation-state, the quest for cultural self-determination precedes the quest for political self-determination and prepares the ground for the latter. This was the case with most central and eastern European peoples in the nineteenth century and is the case with the Arabs in the twentieth century. Nationalism, from the early nineteenth century on, carried with it the demand for 'national' or 'popular' foundations for all cultural and intellectual life. This process began with the decline of supra-national and theoretically universal cultural elements, such as the founding of all Western education on a thorough and often exclusive training in the classical languages; the role of French as the language of diplomacy and international relations; the erudition in Arabic in all Islamic countries; the exclusive use of classical Chinese as the literary language until Hu Shih's language revolution in 1917. These elements were replaced by an entirely new emphasis on the vernacular, on the political prestige of the national language, on folklore and folk traditions, and on the accessibility of culture to the non-learned classes.

Such a demand for cultural nationalism, which in its extreme cases parallels the demand for absolute political sovereignty and self-sufficiency, could also be found in United States nationalism, although it conflicted there with the more cosmopolitan trends of the Enlightenment, the age in which the United States became a nation. Noah Webster, in his *Sketches of American Policy*, wrote: 'America is an independent empire, and ought to assume a national character. Nothing can be more ridiculous, than a servile imitation of the manners, the language, and the vices of foreigners. For setting aside the infancy of our government and our inability to support the fashionable amusement of Europe, nothing can betray a more despicable disposition in Americans than to be the apes of Europeans' (1785, p. 47).

Walt Whitman, with all his cosmopolitan embraces of mankind, in the *Leaves of Grass*, 1855, could appeal in his dithyrambic way to America: 'Strangle the singers who will not sing you loud and strong! . . . Call for new great masters who comprehend new arts, new perfections, new wants! Submit to the most robust bard till he remedy your barrenness! Then you will not need to adopt the airs of others; you will have true airs, begotted of yourself, blooded with your own blood.' Whitman specifically referred to Johann Gottfried Herder's belief that creative work can be done only in one's 'own' folk language, that great art has always been the expression of and is determined by the 'national' spirit (*Volksgeist*).

In Whitman two fundamental and opposite strains of nationalism confront each other – the one that corresponds to the 'open' society and the one that corresponds to the 'closed' society. No nationalism or phase of nationalism shows one of these strains in purity: it is always a question of emphasis. The 'open' nationalism represents the more 'modern' form: it inclines toward intercourse, and its basis is generally a territorial organization and a political society, constituting a nation of fellow citizens irrespective of race or ethnic descent. The 'closed' nationalism stresses the nation's autochthonous character, the common origins (race, blood) and rootedness in the ancestral soil. These determine the 'purity' of national character and preserve it from 'alien' influences. The romantic, anti-Western, and anti-Enlightenment Germanophilism and Slavophilism of the nineteenth century offer examples of such a 'closed' nationalism; the image of their ideal society was to be found in the tribal or premodern past, in emphasis on *Eigenart* or *samobytnost*. The 'open' nationalism, on the other hand, finds its ideal image in a future that will build bridges over the separations of the past. The 'open' nationalism stresses the free self-determination of the individual; the 'closed' nationalism, biological or historical determinism.

One of the outstanding examples of an 'open' nationalism is provided by the United States. The Americans rejected common descent as the basis of their nationhood. They did not establish their nation on a common past with its roots in antiquity or medieval times, on a common religion or a unique cultural tradition. They owe their nationhood to the affirmation of the modern trends of emancipation, assimilation, mobility, and individualism. They inherited the English tradition of limited and mild government and constitutional freedoms; but the historical rights of Englishmen became, in the climate of the eighteenth-century Enlightenment, universal rights, which, theoretically, had the strength to transform men of the most various pasts and descents into new men, building a common future in a new land.

RACIAL PURITY. Racial purity has often formed the theoretical basis of nationality throughout history. At the time of the building of the second Jewish state, national regeneration implied the repudiation of the wives whom Jews had taken from foreign tribes and of the children whom those wives had borne (Ezra 10; Nehemiah 10.30). Even the State of Israel grants an exclusive, privileged status to persons of Jewish descent in matters of immigration and citizenship. In its most extreme form, racial exclusivism and rootedness in the ancestral soil became the basis of nationhood in National Socialist Germany. The German Reich was regarded as the true homeland and the centre of loyalty of all individuals of German descent, regardless of the 'accident' of their political citizenship or the personal self-determination of their individual allegiance.

The historian Heinrich von Treitschke stressed this point of view as early as 1870 in the case of the Alsatians. The French historian Ernest Renan, in his lecture *Qu'est-ce qu'une nation?* (1882), declared the racial theory 'a very great fallacy whose dominance would ruin European civilization . . . According to this theory the Germans have the right to take back the scattered members of the German family, even if these members [do not wish it]. Thus one creates a primordial right analogous to that of the divine right of Kings. . . . Will the Germans, who have raised the banner of ethnography so high, not see one day the Slavs [follow their example and reclaim the lands] of their ancestors? It is good for all of us to know how to forget' (pp. 1–29, *passim*).

NATIONAL SUPREMACY. The rise of the new nation-states in the nineteenth and twentieth centuries started bitter disputes about frontier territories, as each nationality claimed 'historical' rights according to its greatest historical expansion. Thus, independent Serbia and independent Bulgaria, in spite of their close affinity of language and religion and their common past of subjection to the Turks, faced each other in repeated struggles over Macedonia, which both claimed as having formed part, in long-past times, of their respective empires. The fate of the Slav Ukrainians was involved in the centuries-old fight of their Slav neighbours, the Poles, and the Russians, for hegemony in the eastern borderlands of Europe. Nationalities that had demanded release from oppression often became, after liberation, oppressors themselves, sometimes subjecting others to more severe oppression than they had suffered themselves. Most of the new states, although ethnically mixed, regarded themselves as power instruments of the dominant, or 'state-forming', nationality among the several inhabiting the territory, and denied equality to the other nationalities in 'their' state. This was the case in Poland, Czechoslovakia, and Yugoslavia after World War I, and in Ceylon after World War II. Kurds and Somalis in the 1960s sought national union as the Poles and southern Slavs had done fifty years before. The potentially fruitful innovation of international treaties binding the new nation-states after 1918 to protect national minorities, under the League of Nations, did not become effective. On the other hand, the expulsion or shift of populations from their homelands for nationalistic reasons, first envisaged by the Germans in World War I in order to annex lands 'without people' for German settlement and strategic purposes, became widespread in the twentieth century. Nationalism has 'solved' many tensions; it has at the same time created new ones, in which modern aspirations and age-old memories are often inextricably mixed.

Some of the fundamental beliefs of nationalism go far back in history. Among them are the 'chosen people' idea and the 'promised land' concept. Both originated with the ancient Hebrews; both provided a divine sanction for nationalist aspirations and political aims; both are found in various forms throughout the ages as a conscious or unconscious Biblical heritage. With the advent of Stoicism and Christianity, which became the official creeds of the 'universal' Roman empire, the narrow and 'closed' tribalism of older times was overcome in an ecumenical 'open' society. This universalism survived in the Christian world until the Renaissance and Reformation; in Islam, until the later nineteenth century. In the Western world, the new absolutist states of the post-Renaissance period, with their emphasis on sovereignty, centralization, and *rasion d'etat*, created the political organization that eighteenth-century nationalism began to transform into the modern nation-state. Modern nationalism first took hold in England in the seventeenth century and in Anglo-America in the eighteenth century. But this nationalism respected, and was based upon, the individual liberties and self-government characteristic of the development of these nations. The rise of nationalism in the French Revolution was different. The absolutist and centralized French monarchy had set the example for continental Europe in the seventeenth and eighteenth centuries; the nationalism of the French people continued this form and set the model for the centralized European nation-state of the nineteenth century. The Napoleonic wars carried the aggressiveness of the new nationalism to the four corners of Europe.

The European revolutions of 1848/1849 and the defeat of their liberal aspirations marked the spread of nationalism to central and central-eastern Europe, the 'awakening' of the peoples. The striving for individual liberty was drowned in the rising tide of national (collective) self-assertion and will to power. John Stuart Mill complained in 1849 that nationalism makes men indifferent to the rights and interests 'of any portion of the human species save that which is called by the same name, and speaks the same language, as themselves' ([1849] 1865, p. 53). He called the new exclusive nationalism, with its appeal to historical rights, barbaric and remarked bitterly that 'in the backward parts of Europe, and even (where better things might have been expected) in Germany, the sentiment of nationality so far outweighs the love of liberty, that the people are willing to abet their rulers in crushing the liberty and independence of any people not of their race and language' (Mill [1849] 1865, p. 53). After 1848 nationalism, originally a movement of emancipation and constitutional rights, became known as *Realpolitik* and *Machtpolitik*. The *sacro egoismo* of nationalism reached its climax in the fascist movements.

The war of 1914, which was started by dynastic empires, partly under popular pressure, replaced the empires with nation-states all over central and east-central Europe. At the same time it helped the spread of nationalism to Asia. Half a century later nationalism had become the dominant force throughout the non-Western world, and the political map of Asia and Africa changed between 1945 and 1965 as completely as had the map of Europe between 1815 and 1920.

In the middle of the twentieth century, nationalism everywhere prevailed over supra-national ideology. Catholic France and Muslim Turkey had made common cause against Catholic Austria. At the end of the nineteenth century, republican France and Czarist Russia were brought together, not by ideological affinity but by the common fear of German aggressiveness and over-confidence. Ideological affinity and historical friendship between the dynastic empires of the Romanovs and Hohenzollerns did not prevail against the rising tide of nationalism. German statesmen characterized the war of 1914 as a struggle between Pan-Germanism and Pan-Slavism for the control of 'Mitteleuropa'. When National Socialist Germany resumed the hegemonial war in 1939, it attacked semi-fascist and anti-Semitic Poland, in spite of ideological affinities and friendship, and destroyed that country in close collaboration with communist Russia. In October 1940, fascist Italy attacked Greece, whose dictator, General John Metaxas, was an outspoken admirer of fascism.

In the ideological blocs of the post-World War II era, nationalist differences made themselves more and more felt. The authoritarian nationalism of de Gaulle's France might be a factor in the disintegration of the democratic West and is reviving the goal of a European third force under French hegemony, independent of both English-speaking democracies and the communist East. Within the communist bloc, conflicting nationalist interests created acute tensions among the Soviet Union, communist China, Yugoslavia, and Albania. The imperialist trends of traditional Russian and Chinese national policies reasserted themselves, modified and rejuvenated by communist ideology. As early as 1948, communist Yugoslavia affirmed and maintained her independence from communist Russia. Moreover, nationalist territorial claims hindered friendly cooperation between Yugoslavia and her two communist neighbours, Albania and Bulgaria. In the early 1960s the monolithic character of international communism was merely an ideological spectre, not a political reality; the communist nations were even farther from a supra-national federative union than were the democracies. Even within the Union of Soviet Socialist Republics there were centrifugal nationalist trends which had been especially marked during the crises of World War II.

Although nationalism remained the *idée-force* after 1945, there were unmistakable trends toward supranational forms of cooperation and political organization. Earlier experiments at integration of closely related nations had not been promising. In the nineteenth century, a strong Pan-Scandinavian movement existed; yet these countries jealously preserved their national sovereignty, policy, and personality, achieving separation (Norway from Sweden; Iceland from Denmark), not integration. The small Central American republics, apparently united by language, religion, and history, tried in vain to federate. After World War II, however, the agitations for a union of the democracies, for European unity, for an Atlantic community, for African unity seemed more promising. Numerous conferences were held; organizations were created whose strength was greater on paper than in reality; and limited progress was achieved, especially in concrete economic and social legislation and in organized cultural exchange. But even the smaller projects, like Benelux (Belgium, Netherlands, Luxembourg) or the Maghreb (Tunisia, Algeria, Morocco), ran into difficulties once the discussion of desirabilities was to be abandoned for the realization of concrete possibilities. Traditional nationalism and continuing or newly emerging hegemonial claims, coupled with the clashing ambitions of national leaders and the staying power of existing governmental frameworks, strengthened the centrifugal trends among the nations, highly developed and less developed, 'old' and 'new'.

The comparative study of nationalism will not reveal any fundamental differences between 'old' and 'new' forms of nationalism or between nationalism in the Western and non-Western worlds. Significant discrepancies exist everywhere, but they are more specific and individual than generic. On the whole, the 'new' nations show trends and problems similar to those shown by the 'new' nations of central Europe in the nineteenth century and of east-central Europe in the early twentieth century. Some of these 'Western' nations in central-eastern and southern Europe were at the time of their rise to nationhood, and for decades thereafter, economically and socially under-developed, preserving much of their pre-modern 'feudal' or medieval character. The Latin American nations are 'old' as far as the history of national statehood goes, but in their social backwardness many resemble the 'new' nations of the middle of the twentieth century. All these nations bear witness to the profound transformation that is being brought about by world-wide trends: the possibilities of, and desire for, rapid technologi-cal change; the experience of such radical and violent move-ments as communism and fascism; the demand for social equali-ty and for the active participation of the masses in national life; the 'population explosion' and the growth of giant cities. In this transformation, which increases global uniformity, nation-alism acts as an accelerating factor because the policies of the newer or less developed nation-states have often been guided by the desire to catch up with the older and more highly de-veloped nation-states. Nationalism can, however, also act as a force preserving older forms of societal life and stressing the diversity within a world community that is based on the accept-ance of the nation-state as the basic form of political and cul-tural organization.

Nationalism and the nation-state form the recognized found-ation of the international organizations of the mid-twentieth century. The United Nations reflects in its growth the dynamic changes brought about by nationalism in the years after World War II. It has successfully smoothed the transition of many colonies to national statehood, a transition that had, in the past, frequently been accompanied by violent civil wars and protract-ed unrest. The United Nations accepted the principle of the legal equality of small and great nations and provided each with a voice in world affairs, thereby contradicting the attitude of the nineteenth-century Concert of Great Powers and rejecting the twentieth-century fascist disregard for the rights of 'weak' or 'small' states. The clashing interests of nations found in the United Nations a forum in which, for the first time in history, all people, civilizations, and ideologies could meet and discuss their differences according to the procedures developed by Western parliamentary traditions. The United Nations represents a hope of divesting clashing nationalist aspirations of their extremist character while recognizing their intrinsic validity. It also helps to intensify the peaceful intercourse among nations by creating and maintaining the outward forms of equality of status.

It is difficult to foresee the future of nationalism. It is a divisive force in a world growing more and more interdependent, a force capable of producing bitter tensions and one-sided, self-righteous judgments that threaten the rational solution of international conflicts. On the other hand, nationalism is an important factor in preventing any one or two of the strongest powers from establishing their hegemony over the whole globe or over a large part of it. In that respect, nationalism is a form of resistance to imposed uniformity, a bulwark of the beneficial diversity, individuality, and liberty of collective groups. It may be that in the future an attitude of tolerance and coexistence will divest the various forms of nationalism of the aggressive political power drive that has characterized the age of nationalism. The growing fear of the consequences of an armed conflict may help to bring about such a change of attitude. In the 1960s the fear of war was powerful in all European nations, even those which welcomed previous wars. Incidents that in the nineteenth century would have led to war no longer play such a decisive role.

The beginning of a general change of public temper in respect to the role of nationalism and the nation-state in international relations has been noticeable. Some historians have compared this change with the change, brought about by the Enlightenment and the rise of tolerance, that replaced the age of religious wars in Europe with a period of uneasy and distrustful but generally peaceful coexistence of conflicting religions. A long process of change, beginning in the late seventeenth century and taking at least two hundred years, was necessary before this fundamental attitude was generally accepted in the Western world. With the greater acceleration characteristic of the twentieth cenury, a similar process may transform the age of nationalism and of warring nation-states with different civilizations and ideologies into an age of coexistence of free and equal nationalities.